TESTE DEIN WISSEN

Wie gut bin ich in

ENGLISCH

Unregelmäßige Verben

Gisela Mosch

Compact Verlag

Redaktion: Andrea Müh, Heike Mensch, Burkhard Engelmann
Umschlaggestaltung: Inga Koch
Printed in Germany
ISBN: 3-8174-7204-8
7172041

Inhalt

Abkürzungsverzeichnis:

AE	American English/Amerikanisches Englisch
BE	British English/Britisches Englisch
coll.	colloquial/Umgangssprache
cont.	continuous/Verlaufsform
fut.	future tense/Zukunft I
pres.	present tense/Gegenwart
s.o.	someone/jemand
s.p.	simple past/1. Vergangenheit
s.th.	something/etwas
vgl.	vergleiche

Vorwort

Gute Kenntnisse der unregelmäßigen Verben des Englischen sind eine Voraussetzung für den korrekten englischen Sprachgebrauch. Viele von ihnen gehören zum Grundwortschatz und damit zu den am häufigsten gebrauchten Wörtern. Das vorliegende Buch gibt mit **333 Fragen und Antworten** gezielte Hilfen zur Überprüfung und Festigung des eigenen Wissens auf diesem Gebiet.

Im alphabetisch geordneten Aufgabenteil werden zunächst mit Einsetzübungen die Kenntnisse der grammatischen Grundformen geprüft. Weiterhin wird der Umgang mit diesen Formen im Satzzusammenhang trainiert. Darauf folgen Übungen zu Redewendungen. Sie werden erstaunt sein, wie viele von ihnen mit deutschen Redewendungen übereinstimmen.

Ein **Anhang** enthält ergänzend eine Übersicht über unregelmäßige Verben, die nicht behandelt werden, da sie weniger gebräuchlich sind.

Alle Antworten sind im **Lösungsteil** aufgeführt. In farblich hervorgehobenen Merkkästen wird auf Besonderheiten in Gebrauch oder Bedeutung der Verben hingewiesen.

Wie gut bin ich in Englisch - Unregelmäßige Verben ist das ideale Trainingsbuch für alle, die ihr Wissen und Können im Englischen schnell überprüfen und erweitern möchten. Die Übungen können ohne zusätzliche Materialien gelöst werden: Sie brauchen nur einen Stift zur Hand zu nehmen, und schon kann es losgehen.

Viel Erfolg!

awake

Fill in the right form of the verb: / Setzen Sie die korrekte Verbform ein: 1

a) Every morning I _______ at 8 o'clock. (pres.)

b) Last week my dog _______ in the middle of the night and started barking loudly.

Which is the correct sentence? / Welcher Satz ist richtig? 2

a) He awokes his wife with his coughing. ☐

b) He awoke his wife with his coughing. ☐

c) The chicken have awaked long before me today. ☐

d) The chicken have awaken long before me today. ☐

e) The chicken have awoken long before me today. ☐

Idioms - do you know their meaning? / Redewendungen - kennen Sie ihre Bedeutung? 3

a) to awake to s.th. ________________________________

The gangster *awoke to the fact* that he would never escape the police.

b) to awake s.o. to s.th. ________________________________

The teacher *awoke me to my faults.*

be

Form meaningful sentences: / Bilden Sie sinnvolle Sätze: 4

a) The school this girl went to	has been	a very traditional one.
b) My grandmother	was	wonderful, she sends me a letter each week.
c) This theatre performance	is	the best I have seen so far.

5 **Fill in the right form of the verb: / Setzen Sie die korrekte Verbform ein:**

a) Today, the weather ____ very fine.

b) I used to be a good athlete when I ____ young.

c) I told him that I had ____ so angry that I had thrown his present away.

6 **Idioms - do you know their meaning? / Redewendungen - kennen Sie ihre Bedeutung?**

a) to be about to do s.th. ____________________

b) to be all ears ____________________

c) to be in one's right mind ____________________

d) to be in the picture ____________________

e) to be on the safe side ____________________

beat

7 **Fill in the right form of the verb: / Setzen Sie die korrekte Verbform ein:**

a) Usually, the better team ______ the other one. (pres.)

b) I _____ the eggwhite until it became stiff.

c) This child has never been ______ by its parents.

8 **Which is the correct sentence? / Welcher Satz ist richtig?**

a) The man has beated his dog because he had run away. ☐

b) The man has beaten his dog because he had run away. ☐

c) In a sportsgame the winner beats the loser. ☐

d) In a sportsgame the winner beaten the loser. ☐

9 **Idioms - do you know their meaning? / Redewendungen - kennen Sie ihre Bedeutung?**

a) Can you beat it? ____________________

b) That beats everything! ____________________

c) to beat about the bush ____________________

d) to beat the deadline ____________________

become

Fill in the right form of the verb: / Setzen Sie die korrekte Verbform ein: 10

a) The little boy wants to ____ a filmstar one day.

b) She _________ very angry when she saw the mess.

c) The shoes have _______ old over the last year.

Cross out the wrong forms: / Streichen Sie die falschen Verbformen durch: 11

a) The floor become/becomes dirty when you walk on it with muddy boots.

b) His work became/becamed more and more difficult.

c) After her long studies she has became/become a doctor, finally.

An idiom - do you know its meaning? / Eine Redewendung - kennen Sie ihre Bedeutung? 12

to become the rule ____

It has *become the rule* that everyone put away their own dirty plates.

begin

Fill in the right form of the verb: / Setzen Sie die korrekte Verbform ein: 13

a) Are you sitting comfortably? Then we can ________ .

b) Richard ______ to sing right after the lesson had come to an end.

c) Has he ever _____ his work on time?

Cross out the wrong forms: / Streichen Sie die falschen Verbformen durch: 14

a) We will begin/begine painting as soon as the walls have dried off.

b) When their parents left the children began/begun to prepare for the party.

c) Not only had they begun/began to roll up the carpets, they had also begun to drag away the rest of the furniture.

15 **Idioms - do you know their meaning? / Redewendungen - kennen Sie ihre Bedeutung?**

a) to begin with, . . . ________________

Well, *to begin with*, I'd like to introduce you to the director of our firm.

b) well begun is half done ________________

My dad prays every morning as he believes that *well begun is half done*.

c) to begin on s.th. ________________

With this sentence on her lips she would *begin on anything*.

bend

16 **Fill in the right form of the verb: / Setzen Sie die korrekte Verbform ein:**

a) You must __________ your knees when you ski.

b) He __________ the iron bar as if it were a piece of wire.

c) He had ___________ many branches away from the path.

17 **Which is the correct sentence? / Welcher Satz ist richtig?**

a) The teacher bent down to pick up the chalk. ☐

b) The teacher bents down to pick up the chalk. ☐

c) Her head had been bent in sorrow from the day he left. ☐

d) Her head had been bend in sorrow from the day he left. ☐

18 **Idioms - do you know their meaning? / Redewendungen - kennen Sie ihre Bedeutung?**

a) to bend one's knee ________________

b) to bend oneself to a task ________________

c) to bend out of shape ________________

d) to bend over backwards to do s.th. ________________

bet

Fill in the right form of the verb: / Setzen Sie die korrekte Verbform ein: 19

a) I _____ that the black horse will win the race.

b) Yesterday we _______ that it would rain today.

c) This cannot be ______ on.

Cross out the wrong forms: / Streichen Sie die falschen Verbformen durch: 20

a) I bet/betted you twenty pounds that I will beat you at golf next time.

b) Everybody betted/bets/bet on the same horse.

Idioms - do you know their meaning? / Redewendungen - kennen Sie ihre Bedeutung? 21

a) You bet! ______________________________

b) You can bet your bottom dollar on that! ______________________________

bind

Fill in the right form of the verb: / Setzen Sie die korrekte Verbform ein: 22

a) She always ________ her hair up in a pigtail. (pres.)

b) They ________ the book with great care. (s.p.)

c) The hostage was ________ to the chair so that he could not move.

Which is the correct sentence? / Welcher Satz ist richtig? 23

a) All the members of our club must be bound to secrecy. ☐

b) All the members of our club must be bind to secrecy. ☐

24 **Idioms - do you know their meaning? / Redewendungen - kennen Sie ihre Bedeutung?**

a) to be bound to do s.th. ______________________

He is *bound to do something* silly. ______________________

b) That was bound to happen. ______________________

c) *I'm bound to say* that I don't believe it. ______________________

d) to be bound up in s.th. ______________________

One can see that he *is bound up in something* important. ____________

____

bite

25 **Fill in the right form of the verb: / Setzen Sie die korrekte Verbform ein:**

a) Snoopy, my dog, _______ me tenderly each time I come home.

b) When grandpa _________ into an apple he lost his last tooth.

c) His best cowboy has never been ________ by a snake.

26 **Cross out the wrong forms: / Streichen Sie die falschen Verbformen durch:**

a) He spent hours fishing but nothing would ever bit/bite.

b) Heavy smoke was biting/bitting my eyes.

c) His face looked terrible - it was badly bit/bitten by the mosquitoes.

27 **Idioms - do you know their meaning? / Redewendungen - kennen Sie ihre Bedeutung?**

a) to bite back a remark ______________________

b) to bite the dust ______________________

c) to bite one's lips ______________________

d) the biter will be bitten ______________________

e) once bitten, twice shy ______________________

bleed

Fill in the right form of the verb: / Setzen Sie die korrekte Verbform ein: 28

a) Bleeders _____ easily and do not stop.

b) When my sister was small her nose ________ every day.

c) He would have ____________ to death if the doctor hadn't come in time.

Cross out the wrong forms: / Streichen Sie die falschen Verbformen durch: 29

a) The wound bled/bleeds so badly that she fainted.

b) Ronald has cut his finger; now it is bleding/bleeding badly.

Idioms - do you know their meaning? / Redewendungen - kennen Sie ihre Bedeutung? 30

a) my heart bleeds for you ____

b) to bleed for something ____

c) to bleed someone white ____

blow

Fill in the right form of the verb: / Setzen Sie die korrekte Verbform ein: 31

a) The wind __________ in the Sahara desert. (pres.)

b) On her last birthday she _________ out all the thirty candles on her cake with one breath.

c) Diane had _________ her nose so often that she didn't have any tissues left.

Form meaningful sentences: / Bilden Sie sinnvolle Sätze: 32

a) She had a cold and	blow	her nose all the time.
b) The storm has finally	blew	over; it has taken down our roof.
c) Could you please	blown	the candle out?

33 **Idioms - do you know their meaning? / Redewendungen - kennen Sie ihre Bedeutung?**

a) to blow hot and cold ______________________________

b) to blow off steam ______________________________

c) to blow one's top ______________________________

d) to blow up ______________________________

e) to blow s.th. up ______________________________

break

34 **Fill in the right form of the verb: / Setzen Sie die korrekte Verbform ein:**

a) While his father tries to wash the dishes the little son tries to ________ them.

b) Her heavy blows finally _______ the ice. (s.p.)

c) He is a passionated skier, although he has _______ his leg already twice.

35 **Which is the correct sentence? / Welcher Satz ist richtig?**

a) She bumped against the shelf so that five wineglasses got broke. ☐

b) She bumped against the shelf so that five wineglasses broke. ☐

c) We were very disappointed with our friends because they had broken their word. ☐

d) We were very disappointed with our friends because they had broke their word. ☐

36 **Idioms - do you know their meaning? / Redewendungen - kennen Sie ihre Bedeutung?**

a) to break the ice ______________________________

Her funny remark *broke the ice*. ______________________________

b) to break new ground ______________________________

c) to break the news to s.o. ______________________________

We had *to break the news* of his accident to his parents. ______________

d) to break up a relationship ______________________________

bring

Fill in the right form of the verb: / Setzen Sie die korrekte Verbform ein: 37

a) Please, ______ me the salt from the kitchen, will you?

b) On my wedding they even ______ the dog. (s.p.)

c) This little stone has ______ me good luck.

Cross out the wrong forms: / Streichen Sie die falschen Verbformen durch: 38

a) As she hasn't brought/bringed back the car I can't drive home yet.

b) Come and bring/brought your friends along with you.

c) Their conversation brought/broughts him down to earth.

Idioms - do you know their meaning? / Redewendungen - kennen Sie ihre Bedeutung? 39

a) to bring s.o. to his senses ______________________________

b) to bring s.o. down to earth ______________________________

c) to bring about a change ______________________________

d) to bring s.th. up ______________________________

e) to bring the house down ______________________________

f) to bring s.th. to light ______________________________

g) to bring s.o. down ______________________________

h) to bring s.th. into play ______________________________

i) to bring s.th. into the open ______________________________

build

Fill in the right form of the verb: / Setzen Sie die korrekte Verbform ein: 40

a) I've always wanted to ________ a treehouse high up in the branches

b) Their relationship was ________ on sand; it had to fail.

c) Near our cottage a new railway has been __________ .

41 **Form meaningful sentences: / Bilden Sie sinnvolle Sätze:**

a) The Eskimo boy has	build	the igloo out of icy blocks of snow.
b) Do not	built	on him, he never does what he says.
c) Rome wasn't	built	in a day.

42 **Idioms - do you know their meaning? / Redewendungen - kennen Sie ihre Bedeutung?**

a) to build one's hopes on ______________________

b) to build castles in the air ______________________

c) built on sand ______________________

burn

43 **Fill in the right form of the verb: / Setzen Sie die korrekte Verbform ein:**

a) Dry logs ________ better than wet logs. (pres.)

b) The husband ________ his fingers on the hot oven. (s.p.)

c) The parents hoped that their children hadn't ___________ the house down.

44 **Cross out the wrong forms: / Streichen Sie die falschen Verbformen durch:**

a) In poor countries people burn/burne their rubbish in their backyards.

b) In India the dead have always been burnd/burnt/burned.

c) At Easter we lit a big bonfire and burnt/burn/burned lots of dry brambles.

45 **Idioms - do you know their meaning? / Redewendungen - kennen Sie ihre Bedeutung?**

a) to burn one's boats ______________________

b) to burn the midnight oil ______________________

c) to burn the candle at both ends ______________________________

d) to burn to the ground ______________________________________

burst

Fill in the right form of the verb: / Setzen Sie die korrekte Verbform ein: 46

a) He always __________ into the room without knocking. (pres.)

b) The red balloon __________ first. (s.p.)

c) I would have ____________ if I had eaten another piece of that cake.

Form meaningful sentences: / Bilden Sie sinnvolle Sätze: 47

a) Suddenly my mother	bursts	into the room.
b) With the exam in my hand I was	burst	with pride.
c) He is so fat that he	bursting	out of his jeans.

Idioms - do you know their meaning? / Redewendungen - kennen Sie ihre Bedeutung? 48

a) to burst into flames ______________________________________

b) to burst into laughter/tears ________________________________

c) to burst into leaf ____

d) to burst with laughter ____________________________________

e) to burst with pride _______________________________________

f) to burst with energy ______________________________________

buy

Fill in the right form of the verb: / Setzen Sie die korrekte Verbform ein: 49

a) I will ________ the tickets for the concert tomorrow morning.

b) My aunt ________ me such a nice birthday present. (s.p.)

c) This beautiful table was ________ in England.

50 **Which is the correct sentence? / Welcher Satz ist richtig?**

a) He bought the house from his best friend. ☐

b) He buyed the house from his best friend. ☐

c) I have forgotten to bought some milk. ☐

d) I have forgotten to buy some milk. ☐

51 **Idioms - do you know their meaning? / Redewendungen - kennen Sie ihre Bedeutung?**

a) to buy time ____________________

By talking a lot of nonsense he tried *to buy time*. ____________

b) to buy s.th. for a song ____________________

c) I don't buy that! ____________________

catch

52 **Fill in the right form of the verb: / Setzen Sie die korrekte Verbform ein:**

a) If you want to ________ a mouse, you have to be very quick.

b) The girl was so fast that her friend never ________ her.

c) The police have ________ the escaped criminal already.

53 **Form meaningful sentences: / Bilden Sie sinnvolle Sätze:**

a) At last I	catch	up with her.
b) My uncle always	caught	many fish during his holidays.
c) Are you able to	catches	a very fast ball well?

54 **Idioms - do you know their meaning? / Redewendungen - kennen Sie ihre Bedeutung?**

a) to catch s.o. red-handed ____________________

b) to catch s.o.'s eye ____________________

c) to catch one's breath ____________________

d) to catch sight of s.o. ____________________

e) to catch up with s.o. ____________________

choose

Fill in the right form of the verb: / Setzen Sie die korrekte Verbform ein: 55

a) What would you like for your birthday? You can ________ what you want.

b) Are you sure you ________ the right woman to be your wife? (s.p.)

c) Yes, of course I have ________ the right one. I love her.

Cross out the wrong forms: / Streichen Sie die falschen Verbformen durch: 56

a) I have chosen/choosen a green dress to wear at the wedding.

b) The children chose/choose to stay indoors since the wheather was so bad.

c) Freddy seldom chooses/choses a different restaurant.

Idioms - do you know their meaning? / Redewendungen - kennen Sie ihre Bedeutung? 57

a) Do as you choose! ________________________________

b) There is not much to choose between them ________________

c) We cannot choose but do it ________________________

come

Fill in the right form of the verb: / Setzen Sie die korrekte Verbform ein: 58

a) ______ to our house on Christmas!

b) He was so sad because she never _______ back.

c) I'm glad that summer has finally _______ .

Which is the correct sentence? / Welcher Satz ist richtig? 59

a) Daddy, will Father Christmas come to us again this year? ☐

b) Daddy, will Father Christmas comes to us again this year? ☐

60 **Idioms - do you know their meaning? / Redewendungen - kennen Sie ihre Bedeutung?**

a) to come about ______________________
b) to come round ______________________
c) to come in handy ______________________
d) to come into fashion ______________________
e) to come off ______________________
f) to come to grips with s.th. ______________________
g) to come to the conclusion that ______________________
h) to come to one's senses ______________________
i) to come to the point ______________________
j) to come to terms with s.o. ______________________
k) to come to terms with s.th. ______________________
l) to come under fire ______________________
m) to come up with s.th. ______________________
n) come to think of it... ______________________
o) come what may ______________________
p) in the years to come ______________________
q) Come off it! ______________________

cost

61 **Fill in the right form of the verb: / Setzen Sie die korrekte Verbform ein:**

a) The wonderful velvet hat ________ only a few pounds. (pres.)
b) It ________ an awful lot to redecorate (renovieren) this house. (s.p.)
c) It has ________ my father a lot of time to prepare this delicious meal.

62 **Cross out the wrong forms: / Streichen Sie die falschen Verbformen durch:**

a) This is a nice shirt. How much does it costs/cost?
b) Writing this book costs/costed me much time.
c) His fancy for fast cars has cost/costed him his life.

Idioms - do you know their meaning? / Redewendungen - kennen Sie ihre Bedeutung? 63

a) to cost s.o. dearly ______________________________

b) to cost the earth ______________________________

c) to cost an arm and a leg ______________________________

creep

Fill in the right form of the verb: / Setzen Sie die korrekte Verbform ein: 64

a) The naughty girl tries to ________ out of the house.

b) I dropped some money so I ________under the table to pick it up again. (s.p.)

c) A beetle has ________ over the path.

Form meaningful sentences: / Bilden Sie sinnvolle Sätze: 65

a) He	crept	the last few steps.
b) It made my flesh	crept	over the creaking boards.
c) Due to exhaustion I	creep	to watch this movie.

Idioms - do you know their meaning? / Redewendungen - kennen Sie ihre Bedeutung? 66

a) to make s.o.'s flesh creep ______________________________

b) to creep into s.o.'s favour ______________________________

c) to creep over s.o. ______________________________

d) to creep up ______________________________

e) to creep up on s.o. ______________________________

f) to creep back ______________________________

g) time creeps on ______________________________

cut

67 **Fill in the right form of the verb: / Setzen Sie die korrekte Verbform ein:**

a) All the guests have arrived, you can ______ your birthday-cake now.

b) Dad ______ his finger badly when he tried to sharpen our knives. (s.p.)

c) The front lawn was ______ only yesterday.

68 **Cross out the wrong forms: / Streichen Sie die falschen Verbformen durch:**

a) Mary needs to have her hair cutted/cut.

b) You have to cut/cud this piece of cardboard in two. It's too big.

69 **Idioms - do you know their meaning? / Redewendungen - kennen Sie ihre Bedeutung?**

a) to cut s.th. down ______________________________

b) to cut corners ______________________________

c) to cut one's coat according to one's cloth ______________________________

d) to cut a long story short ______________________________

e) to cut both ways ______________________________

f) Cut it out! ______________________________

g) to cut s.o. dead ______________________________

h) to cut s.o. to the heart ______________________________

i) to cut s.o. down to size ______________________________

j) to cut s.o. off without a penny ______________________________

k) to be cut out for s.th. ______________________________

l) to cut the ground under s.o.'s feet ______________________________

m) to cut s.o. under ______________________________

deal

Fill in the right form of the verb: / Setzen Sie die korrekte Verbform ein: 70

a) The travelling salesman ________ in carpets and paint. (pres.)

b) Last time you ________ the cards you must have cheated.

Which is the correct sentence? / Welcher Satz ist richtig? 71

a) My sister's shop deal in cowboy boots. ☐

b) My sister's shop deals in cowboy boots. ☐

Idioms - do you know their meaning? / Redewendungen - kennen Sie ihre Bedeutung? 72

a) to deal cards ________________________________

Could you *deal the cards* just a little faster, please.

b) to deal with s.o. ________________________________

She felt so unwell in his presence that she never wanted *to deal with him* again.

c) to deal with s.th. ________________________________

He *deals with this* very expertly.

dig

Fill in the right form of the verb: / Setzen Sie die korrekte Verbform ein: 73

a) Stop ________ that hole, it is deep enough.

b) My little brother ________ that hole to see whether there was a treasure hidden in the ground.

c) A mole has ________ up our whole flower bed.

Which is the correct sentence? / Welcher Satz ist richtig? 74

a) In the Sahara you have to dug very deep to find water. ☐

b) In the Sahara you have to dig very deep to find water. ☐

c) He has been digging up the whole garden for me. ☐

d) He has been dug up the whole garden for me. ☐

75 **Idioms - do you know their meaning? / Redewendungen - kennen Sie ihre Bedeutung?**

a) He dug his own grave. ______________________________

b) to dig s.th. up ______________________________

c) Dig in! ______________________________

dive

76 **Fill in the right form of the verb: / Setzen Sie die korrekte Verbform ein:**

a) To find such pearls you have to ________ deep down to the coral reefs.

b) Mum ________ into the water before I came.

c) Dad has never ________ in his whole life.

77 **Cross out the wrong forms: / Streichen Sie die falschen Verbformen durch:**

a) The girl had lost an earring in the swimming pool and five boys dived/doved/dove into the water to find it for her.

b) How deep can you dove/dive?

78 **Idioms - do you know their meaning? / Redewendungen - kennen Sie ihre Bedeutung?**

a) Dive in! ______________________________

b) to dive into the crowd ______________________________

The handsome man *dived/dove into the crowd* and vanished from my sight.

c) to dive for the ball ______________________________

The goalkeeper *dived/dove for the ball* but couldn't catch it anymore.

do

Fill in the right form of the verb: / Setzen Sie die korrekte Verbform ein: 79

a) What will you _______ tomorrow?

b) She was not successful although she _______ her best.

c) I don't know what I have _______ to make her so angry.

Form meaningful sentences: / Bilden Sie sinnvolle Sätze: 80

a) Can you	done	it's how she did it that annoys me.
b) It's not what she	do	anything about it?
c) What have I	did,	that he treats me like this?

Idioms - do you know their meaning? / Redewendungen - kennen Sie ihre Bedeutung? 81

a) to do away with s.th. ______________________________

b) to do business with s.o. ______________________________

c) to do one's bit ______________________________

d) I could do with s.th. ______________________________

e) to do s.o. a favour ______________________________

f) to do s.o. harm ______________________________

g) to do s.o. in ______________________________

h) to be done for ______________________________

i) to do without s.th. ______________________________

j) to do justice to s.o./s.th. ______________________________

k) to do the dishes ______________________________

l) to do oneself up ______________________________

m) to do up one's face ______________________________

n) Nothing doing! ______________________________

o) That will do! ______________________________

draw

82 **Fill in the right form of the verb: / Setzen Sie die korrekte Verbform ein:**

a) Let me help you to _______ a perfect circle.

b) The girls _______ a line which the boys shouldn't step over. (s.p.)

c) So far the dentist has _______ two of her teeth.

83 **Form meaningful sentences: / Bilden Sie sinnvolle Sätze:**

a) Sometimes donkeys still	drawn	the plough.
b) Before he	draw	the tiger he watched him for hours.
c) I thank you for having	drew	my portrait so nicely.

84 **Idioms - do you know their meaning? / Redewendungen - kennen Sie ihre Bedeutung?**

a) to draw alongside ____________________

b) to draw apart ____________________

c) to draw s.o.'s attention to s.th. ____________________

d) to draw s.th. to a close ____________________

e) to draw on s.th. ____________________

f) to draw a cheque ____________________

g) to draw the line at s.th. ____________________

h) to draw near ____________________

dream

85 **Fill in the right form of the verb: / Setzen Sie die korrekte Verbform ein:**

a) Look, she seems to _______ with her eyes open.

b) The old lady _______ of times long past. (s.p.)

c) I have _______ about you the whole night.

Which is the correct sentence? / Welcher Satz ist richtig? 86

a) She never dreamed of seeing him again. He had been gone so long. ☐
b) She never dreamd of seeing him again. He had been gone so long. ☐
c) She never dreamt of seeing him again. He had been gone so long. ☐
d) In some nights I dreams of the loveliest places. ☐
e) In some nights I dream of the loveliest places. ☐
f) He must have dreamed with his eyes open. ☐
g) He must have dreamd with his eyes open. ☐
h) He must have dreamt with his eyes open. ☐

Idioms - do you know their meaning? / Redewendungen - kennen Sie ihre Bedeutung? 87

a) to dream away the hours/the time ______________________________
b) to dream s.th. up ______________________________

drink

Fill in the right form of the verb: / Setzen Sie die korrekte Verbform ein: 88

a) He ________ too much. I think he is an alcoholic. (pres.)
b) The sun had made them so thirsty that they ________ two bottles of water.
c) Jane's dog has ________ water from the river.

Form meaningful sentences: / Bilden Sie sinnvolle Sätze: 89

a) With a fever you should	drink	five cups already.
b) All the guests	drunk	a lot of herb tea.
c) No more coffee for me. I have	drank	to the couple's health.

Idioms - do you know their meaning? / Redewendungen - kennen Sie ihre Bedeutung? 90

a) to drink s.th. away ______________________________
b) to drink s.o. under the table ______________________________

c) to drink in s.o.'s words ______________________________

d) to drink in the air ______________________________

e) to drink in the view ______________________________

drive

91 **Fill in the right form of the verb: / Setzen Sie die korrekte Verbform ein:**

a) ________ carefully because the road is frozen.

b) The heavy wind ________ the clouds away. (s.p.)

c) I have ________ a car before I had a driving license.

92 **Form meaningful sentences: / Bilden Sie sinnvolle Sätze:**

a) Most people here learn to	driven	the nail into the wall.
b) When my sister moved I	drive	at 18.
c) He had finally	drove	the van.

93 **Idioms - do you know their meaning? / Redewendungen - kennen Sie ihre Bedeutung?**

a) to drive s.o. nuts ______________________________

b) to drive s.o. crazy/mad ______________________________

c) to drive s.o. around the bend ______________________________

d) to drive s.th. home to s.o. ______________________________

e) to be driving at s.th. ______________________________

f) drive into a corner ______________________________

eat

94 **Fill in the right form of the verb: / Setzen Sie die korrekte Verbform ein:**

a) I like to ________ Indian food.

b) Each one of us ________ one huge pizza. (s.p.)

c) He has ________ so much that he has gained weight.

Form meaningful sentences: / Bilden Sie sinnvolle Sätze: 95

a) I can't possibly	eaten	at a very fine restaurant on her birthday.
b) They	eat	another piece of cake, thank you.
c) My father has	ate	his favourite meal – potato soup.

Idioms - do you know their meaning? / Redewendungen - kennen Sie ihre Bedeutung? 96

a) to eat like a sparrow/bird ______________________

b) to eat like a horse ______________________

c) to eat one's hat ______________________

d) to eat one's words ______________________

e) to eat out ______________________

f) What's eating him? ______________________

fall

Fill in the right form of the verb: / Setzen Sie die korrekte Verbform ein: 97

a) The temperature will ________ 10 degrees tomorrow night.

b) Grandmother slipped and ________ down the stairs.

c) He has ________ off the horse but he didn't break a bone.

Cross out the wrong forms: / Streichen Sie die falschen Verbformen durch: 98

a) Try not to fall/falls on your knees when you go skating.

b) He fall/fell for her at the very first sight.

c) The temperature of all the sick children has fellen/fallen.

Idioms - do you know their meaning? / Redewendungen - kennen Sie ihre Bedeutung? 99

a) to fall in love with s.o. ______________________

b) to fall for s.o. ______________________

c) to fall through ______________________

d) to fall flat ______________________

e) to fall back on s.th. ______________________

f) to fall behind s.o. ______________________

g) to fall over oneself to do s.th. ______________________

feed

100 **Fill in the right form of the verb: / Setzen Sie die korrekte Verbform ein:**

a) James ________ the chicken every morning. (pres.)

b) They took old bread to the park and ________ the ducks there.

c) Their little son can't eat alone yet. He has to be ________.

101 **Which is the correct sentence? / Welcher Satz ist richtig?**

a) She is so fed up with her living situation that she will move soon. ☐

b) She is so feds up with her living situation that she will move soon. ☐

c) Animals need to be feed every day. ☐

d) Animals need to be fed every day. ☐

e) Will you feed the cats or shall I do it? ☐

f) Will you fed the cats or shall I do it? ☐

102 **Idioms - do you know their meaning? / Redewendungen - kennen Sie ihre Bedeutung?**

a) to breast feed ______________________

b) to feed on s.th. ______________________

c) to feed one's eyes on s.th. ______________________

d) to be fed up with s.th./s.o. ______________________

I hope she leaves pretty soon. I'm really *fed up with her*.

e) to bite the hand that feeds you ______________________

feel

Fill in the right form of the verb: / Setzen Sie die korrekte Verbform ein: 103

a) Can you ________ the warmth of the sun on your belly? It's wonderful.

b) After a shower and a good meal the fugitives ________ a lot better. (s.p.)

c) They had never ________ so happy in their lives.

Cross out the wrong forms: / Streichen Sie die falschen Verbformen durch: 104

a) She could feel/fel the snake gliding over her foot.

b) My brother felt/feld around for his glasses. Without them he couldn't see a thing.

c) I have felt/feeld the earth move under my feet.

Idioms - do you know their meaning? / Redewendungen - kennen Sie ihre Bedeutung? 105

a) to feel like doing s.th. ________________________________

b) to feel up to s.th. ________________________________

c) to feel out of place ________________________________

d) to feel one's way ________________________________

e) to feel sorry for s.o. ________________________________

fight

Fill in the right form of the verb: / Setzen Sie die korrekte Verbform ein: 106

a) He was determined to ________ his way through.

b) The two big dogs ________ fiercely over the bone. (s.p.)

c) She had ________ for her rights before. She knew she could win.

107 **Cross out the wrong forms: / Streichen Sie die falschen Verbformen durch:**

a) Why do we always fight/fought over unimportant things?

b) I think that fighting/fights is boring.

c) The children fought/foughted over the doll.

108 **Idioms - do you know their meaning? / Redewendungen - kennen Sie ihre Bedeutung?**

a) to fight it out ______________________________

b) to fight back one's tears ______________________________

c) to fight a losing battle ______________________________

d) to fight tooth and nail to do s.th. ______________________________

e) to fight one's way ______________________________

find

109 **Fill in the right form of the verb: / Setzen Sie die korrekte Verbform ein:**

a) Look carefully! You will ________ your wedding-ring in the end.

b) Yesterday I ________ a purse with lots of money in it.

c) Peter has just ________ out that he has failed the test.

110 **Which is the correct sentence? / Welcher Satz ist richtig?**

a) Where have you finded her? ☐

b) Where have you found her? ☐

c) Find yourself a husband and settle down, he told me. ☐

d) Found yourself a husband and settle down, he told me. ☐

111 **Idioms - do you know their meaning? / Redewendungen - kennen Sie ihre Bedeutung?**

a) to find s.o. out ______________________________

I *found her out*.

b) to find one's feet ______________________________

He *found his feet*.

c) You must take it as you find it. ______________________

flung

Fill in the right form of the verb: / Setzen Sie die korrekte Verbform ein: 112

a) He always _______ the door open like this when he is in a good mood.

b) As soon as she saw Christoph she shouted with joy and _______ herself into his arms.

c) This naughty little boy has _______ a whole handful of stones at our chicken.

Cross out the wrong forms: / Streichen Sie die falschen Verbformen durch: 113

a) Utterly exhausted Joan flang/flung herself into the chair.

b) Oh, I'm so terribly late. I'm sure she'll fling/flung the flowers back into my face when I finally reach our meeting point.

Idioms - do you know their meaning? / Redewendungen - kennen Sie ihre Bedeutung? 114

a) to fling oneself at someone ______________________

b) to fling something in someone's face ______________________

fly

Fill in the right form of the verb: / Setzen Sie die korrekte Verbform ein: 115

a) Are you able to _______ a plane?

b) Thousands of geese _______ over our heads. They were _______ to Africa. (s.p.; past cont.)

c) I haven't _______ a kite since I was a child.

116 **Form meaningful sentences: - Bilden Sie sinnvolle Sätze:**

a) Tomorrow my best friend will	flown	to England.
b) The birds	fly	away when she clapped her hands.
c) This morning his balloon has	flew	away with the wind.

117 **Idioms - do you know their meaning? / Redewendungen - kennen Sie ihre Bedeutung?**

a) to fly high ______________________________

b) to fly at s.o. ______________________________

c) to fly off the handle ______________________________

d) to let fly at s.o. ______________________________

e) I must fly ______________________________

forbid

118 **Fill in the right form of the verb: / Setzen Sie die korrekte Verbform ein:**

a) My parents always ________ the most interesting things. (pres.)

b) They ________ me to go out dancing last night.

c) I have ________ them to watch TV for a whole week. They have to play games with me, instead.

119 **Form meaningful sentences: / Bilden Sie sinnvolle Sätze:**

a) He	forbidden	you to buy this coat? Why?
b) I	forbade	you to ever meet her again.
c) She has	forbid	her children to play near the road.

120 **Idioms - do you know their meaning? / Redewendungen - kennen Sie ihre Bedeutung?**

a) God forbid that … ______________________________

b) Heaven forbid that … ______________________________

c) God forbid! ______________________________

forget

Fill in the right form of the verb: / Setzen Sie die korrekte Verbform ein: 121

a) He always ________ his hat at our house. (pres.)

b) She ________ to close the door behind her so that it became very cold inside.

c) We have ________ our umbrellas. Now we'll get wet.

Cross out the wrong forms: / Streichen Sie die falschen Verbformen durch: 122

a) You can't have forgotten/forgot the tickets, can you?

b) He promised never to forgotten/forget her no matter how long they would be parted.

c) Let's forget/forgot what happened and start anew, shall we?

Idioms - do you know their meaning? / Redewendungen - kennen Sie ihre Bedeutung? 123

a) to forget oneself____

b) Forget it! ____

c) Forget about it!____

forgive

Form meaningful sentences: / Bilden Sie sinnvolle Sätze: 124

a) She swore never to	forgave	and forgotten the matter long ago.
b) He usually	forgiven	him for this insulting speech.
c) We had	forgive	easily even if one hurt him.

Fill in the right form of the verb: / Setzen Sie die korrekte Verbform ein: 125

a) Please ________ me for saying such a stupid thing.

b) He ________ her at once when he saw the look in her eyes.

c) "It's all ________ and forgotten", she said to her.

126 **An idiom - do you know its meaning? / Eine Redewendung - kennen Sie ihre Bedeutung?**

to forgive s.o. a debt ______________________________

He *forgives her a debt*.

get

127 **Fill in the right form of the verb: / Setzen Sie die korrekte Verbform ein:**

a) Grandfather ________ letters from all over the world. (pres.)

b) The little boy ________ ill from running around with wet trousers on. (s.p.)

c) She has ________ really excited about it.

128 **Which is the correct sentence? / Welcher Satz ist richtig?**

a) My little sister always gets what she wants. ☐

b) My little sister always get what she wants. ☐

c) Look, he has getted her a lovely present. ☐

d) Look, he has gotten her a lovely present. ☐

e) Please, be careful with your sneezing and coughing. I don't want to get the flu as well. ☐

f) Please, be careful with your sneezing and coughing. I don't want to got the flu as well. ☐

129 **Idioms - do you know their meaning? / Redewendungen - kennen Sie ihre Bedeutung?**

a) to get s.th. across ______________________________

b) to get along with s.o. ______________________________

c) to get ahead ______________________________

d) to get carried away ______________________________

e) to get down to business ______________________________

f) to get into a jam ____________________

g) to get into the habit of doing s.th. ____________________

h) to get in touch with s.o. ____________________

i) to get out of hand ____________________

j) to get rid of s.th./s.o. ____________________

k) to get the better of s.th. ____________________

l) to get the better of s.o. ____________________

m) to get the hang of s.th. ____________________

n) to get one's hooks into s.o. ____________________

o) to get on s.o.'s nerves ____________________

p) to get going ____________________

q) to get away with s.th. ____________________

r) to get the sack ____________________

s) to get hold of the wrong end of the stick ____________________

t) to get s.th. over with ____________________

u) How are you? – Well, I get by. ____________________

v) What has gotten into you? ____________________

give

Fill in the right form of the verb: / Setzen Sie die korrekte Verbform ein: 130

a) ________ me a piece of that cake, please.

b) She ________ him her adress so he could write to her. (s.p.)

c) Mum has ________ me a wonderful present for my birthday.

Form meaningful sentences: / Bilden Sie sinnvolle Sätze: 131

a) After the third beer he	give	me the car keys.
b) She has	gave	her a terrible fright.
c) Never	given	up before you have tried everything.

132 **Idioms - do you know their meaning? / Redewendungen - kennen Sie ihre Bedeutung?**

a) to give in to s.o. ______________________________

b) to give s.o. a hand with s.th. ______________________________

c) to give evidence of s.th. ______________________________

d) to give birth to ______________________________

e) to give vent to a feeling ______________________________

f) to give s.th.away (a secret) ______________________________

g) to give s.o. the creeps ______________________________

h) Don't give me that! ______________________________

i) to give rise to ______________________________

j) I don't give a damn about it! ______________________________

k) to give s.o. one's love ______________________________

l) to give s.o. a piece of one's mind ______________________________

m) to give a lecture ______________________________

n) to give the world for s.th. ______________________________

o) to be given up for dead ______________________________

p) to give it to s.o. ______________________________

go

133 **Fill in the right form of the verb: / Setzen Sie die korrekte Verbform ein:**

a) ________ away!

b) Last week we ________ to the cinema twice.

c) The room was empty. He had ________.

134 **Which is the correct sentence? / Welcher Satz ist richtig?**

a) Don't go away! I can't bear to be alone. ☐

b) Don't goe away! I can't bear to be alone. ☐

c) Every day of the summer I went into my garden to watch the plants grow. ☐

d) Every day of the summer I wend into my garden to watch the plants grow. ☐

e) He has not went yet. I can still hear his voice downstairs. ☐

f) He has not gone yet. I can still hear his voice downstairs. ☐

Idioms - do you know their meaning? / Redewendungen - kennen Sie ihre Bedeutung? 135

a) to go about s.th. ______

b) to go awry ______

c) to go Dutch ______

d) to go for a walk ______

e) to go in one ear and out the other ______

f) to go to great trouble/length ______

g) to go to the dogs ______

h) to go along with s.o. ______

i) to go in for s.th. ______

j) to go on and on about s.th. ______

k) to go off the beaten track ______

l) to go out of fashion ______

m) to go with the times ______

n) to go too far ______

o) There you go! ______

p) That goes for all of you. ______

q) That goes without saying. ______

r) Anything goes. ______

grow

Fill in the right form of the verb: / Setzen Sie die korrekte Verbform ein: 136

a) This plant ______ no matter how little water it gets.

b) Where I ______ up there was a big forest behind our house.

c) He has ______ out of these shoes.

137 **Cross out the wrong forms: / Streichen Sie die falschen Verbformen durch:**

a) The puppies growed/grew up so quickly.

b) Grandmother planted these firs 29 years ago. Look, how they have grown/grewn.

c) In this soil everything will grow/grew.

138 **Idioms - do you know their meaning? / Redewendungen - kennen Sie ihre Bedeutung?**

a) to grow old/dark/... ______

b) to grow apart ______

c) to grow away from s.o. ______

d) to grow in numbers ______

e) to grow in wisdom ______

f) to grow into s.o. ______

g) to grow into s.th. ______

h) to grow out of s.th. ______

i) to grow out of a habit ______

j) to grow together ______

k) s.th. grows on s.o. ______

l) Money doesn't grow on trees. ______

have

139 **Fill in the right form of the verb: / Setzen Sie die korrekte Verbform ein:**

a) Do you ________ a dictionary?

b) When I was young I ________ a pony.

c) He has ________ a headache all day long.

140 **Which is the correct sentence? / Welcher Satz ist richtig?**

a) My friend has a lorry we can borrow when we move house. ☐

b) My friend have a lorry we can borrow when we move house. ☐

c) Do you has enough money on you to pay the bill? ☐

d) Do you have enough money on you to pay the bill? ☐

Idioms - do you know their meaning? / Redewendungen - kennen Sie ihre Bedeutung? 141

a) I had better do it. ______________________

b) to have a go at s.th. ______________________

c) to have a try at s.th. ______________________

d) to have a good command of s.th. ______________________

e) to have a crush on s.o. ______________________

f) to have grudge on s.o. ______________________

g) to have a liking for s.o. ______________________

h) to have a say in s.th. ______________________

i) to have a word with s.o. ______________________

j) to have words with s.o. ______________________

k) to have what it takes ______________________

l) to have one's heart in one's mouth ______________________

m) to have a finger in every pie ______________________

n) to have s.th. at one's fingertips ______________________

o) to have one's way ______________________

p) to have the time of one's life ______________________

q) to have it out with s.o. ______________________

r) to have s.th. up one's sleeve ______________________

s) to have many irons in the fire ______________________

t) to have pity on s.o. ______________________

hear

Fill in the right form of the verb: / Setzen Sie die korrekte Verbform ein: 142

a) Our dog is very old. She can no longer ________.

b) They spoke so loud that everybody ________ them.

c) I have ________ someone coming upstairs but there is nobody there now.

143 **Cross out the wrong forms: / Streichen Sie die falschen Verbformen durch:**

a) Have you ever heared/heard such beautiful music?

b) He seems not to hear/hears me. Is he deaf?

c) Grandfather had heard/hearded a child crying and found this little boy sitting all by himself.

144 **Idioms - do you know their meaning? / Redewendungen - kennen Sie ihre Bedeutung?**

a) to hear s.o. out ______________________________

b) to hear from s.o. ______________________________

c) to hear about s.th. ______________________________

d) we would not hear of it ______________________________

hide

145 **Fill in the right form of the verb: / Setzen Sie die korrekte Verbform ein:**

a) If I ________ behind this wall he won't see me.

b) The boy was frightened and ________ his face behind his hands.

c) She has ________ a considerable amount of money somewhere in the house.

146 **Form meaningful sentences: / Bilden Sie sinnvolle Sätze:**

a) Come, let's play	hidden	in this corner and got stuck.
b) Mum has	hide	the easter eggs very well.
c) My brother	hid	and seek!

147 **Idioms - do you know their meaning? / Redewendungen - kennen Sie ihre Bedeutung?**

a) to hide one's feelings ______________________________

Janet never managed *to hide her feelings*.

b) to hide out ______________________________

hit

Fill in the right form of the verb: / Setzen Sie die korrekte Verbform ein: 148

a) If he ever _______ me, I'll leave him at once.

b) He didn't watch out and _______ his head against the wall.

c) He has tried twice and he has _______ the target both times.

Which is the correct sentence? / Welcher Satz ist richtig? 149

a) The pot hit the floor with a loud bang. ☐

b) The pot hid the floor with a loud bang. ☐

c) He hited ten of the nails right on the head and missed only the eleventh. Now he has a blue thumb. ☐

d) He hit ten of the nails right on the head and missed only the eleventh. Now he has a blue thumb. ☐

Idioms - do you know their meaning? / Redewendungen - kennen Sie ihre Bedeutung? 150

a) to hit the nail on the head ____________________

b) to hit it off with s.o. ____________________

c) You have hit it! ____________________

d) to hit the ceiling/roof ____________________

e) to hit the road ____________________

f) to hit back at s.o. ____________________

g) to hit s.o. with a blow ____________________

h) to hit the hay ____________________

hold

Fill in the right form of the verb: / Setzen Sie die korrekte Verbform ein: 151

a) Please, _______ my bag for a moment, I need to have my hands free.

b) She ________ the bunch of roses in her hands. (s.p.)

c) The dogs had been ________ back by the guard as long as possible.

152 **Cross out the wrong forms: / Streichen Sie die falschen Verbformen durch:**

a) All I heard was the operator's voice saying 'Hold/Holds the line...'

b) He helded/held on to the branch for dear life.

c) She had held/holded the baby as if it were made of glass.

153 **Idioms - do you know their meaning? / Redewendungen - kennen Sie ihre Bedeutung?**

a) to hold s.o./s.th. at bay ________

b) to hold one's tongue ________

c) to hold a meeting ________

d) to hold elections ________

e) to hold one's ground ________

f) to hold on to s.th. ________

g) to hold one's breath ________

h) to hold s.o. in high/low esteem ________

i) to hold s.th. cheap ________

j) to hold s.o. responsible ________

k) to hold s.th. against s.o. ________

l) to hold with s.th. ________

m) to hold one's own with s.o. ________

n) to hold s.th. back ________

o) to hold true for ________

p) to hold the view that ________

q) to hold s.o. dear ________

r) not hold water ________

s) Hold the line, please. ________

t) Hold on a minute! ________

u) Hold it! ________

hurt

Fill in the right form of the verb: / Setzen Sie die korrekte Verbform ein: 154

a) It ________ when you comb my hair like this.

b) When he fell from the horse he ________ himself badly.

c) The soldier had been ________ only slightly during the war.

Which is the correct sentence? / Welcher Satz ist richtig? 155

a) This bird can't fly. It must have hurt its wing. ☐

b) This bird can't fly. It must have hurted its wing. ☐

c) By saying these things you hurts me deeply. ☐

d) By saying these things you hurt me deeply. ☐

e) He is such a sweet boy. He couldn't hurt a fly. ☐

f) He is such a sweet boy. He couldn't hurts a fly. ☐

Idioms - do you know their meaning? / Redewendungen - kennen Sie ihre Bedeutung? 156

a) He would not hurt a fly. ________________________________

b) to hurt s.o.'s feelings ________________________________

c) that won't hurt ________________________________

keep

Fill in the right form of the verb: / Setzen Sie die korrekte Verbform ein: 157

a) We are allowed to ________ animals in our flat.

b) All day long he ________ his thoughts to himself. (s.p.)

c) He has ________ the pullover that I lent him and he won't give it back.

Cross out the wrong forms: / Streichen Sie die falschen Verbformen: 158

a) Keeped/Keep your thoughts to yourself. I don't want to hear them.

b) You keeps/keep your pearls locked in the safe, don't you?

c) Have you kept/keeped the group together all the time?

d) My father keeped/kept me away from bad influence as long as he could.

159 **Idioms - do you know their meaning? / Redewendungen - kennen Sie ihre Bedeutung?**

a) to keep at s.th. ____________________

b) to keep up with s.o. ____________________

c) to keep one's fingers crossed ____________________

d) Keep your chin up! ____________________

e) to keep an eye on s.th. ____________________

f) to keep s.o. at arm's length ____________________

g) to keep s.o. at bay ____________________

h) to keep s.th. in mind ____________________

i) to keep in touch with s.o. ____________________

j) to keep on doing s.th. ____________________

k) to keep quiet ____________________

l) to keep s.o. company ____________________

m) to keep track of s.th. ____________________

n) to keep a record of s.th. ____________________

o) to keep out of sight ____________________

p) Keep it up! ____________________

q) to keep s.o. from doing s.th. ____________________

r) to keep up appearances ____________________

s) to keep s.o. waiting ____________________

t) to keep s.o. in the dark about s.th. ____________________

u) to keep cool ____________________

v) to keep clear of s.th. ____________________

w) to keep fit ____________________

x) to keep s.o. in one's place ____________________

y) I won't keep you long ____________________

know

Fill in the right form of the verb: / Setzen Sie die korrekte Verbform ein: 160

a) Do you ________ what time it is?

b) I ________ that he would be late. (s.p.)

c) The couple have ________ one another since they were young.

Form meaningful sentences: / Bilden Sie sinnvolle Sätze: 161

a) I have never	know	a happier person than her.
b) She couldn't	knew	her from somewhere else.
c) He was sure he	known	what would be asked in the exam.

Idioms - do you know their meaning? / Redewendungen - kennen Sie ihre Bedeutung? 162

a) to know s.th. by heart ________________________________

b) to know s.th. inside out ________________________________

c) to be in the know ________________________________

d) to know two things apart ________________________________

e) to know on which side one's bread is buttered________________

f) not that I know of ________________________________

g) as far as I know ________________________________

lay

Fill in the right form of the verb: / Setzen Sie die korrekte Verbform ein: 163

a) Birds ________ their eggs in nests. (pres.)

b) She ________ her hat on the chair. (s.p.)

c) We have ________ the carpet in our bedroom ourselves.

164 **Which is the correct sentence? / Welcher Satz ist richtig?**

a) I lay the blame on him but I was wrong. ☐

b) I laid the blame on him but I was wrong. ☐

c) Would he have lain hands on you? I don't think so. ☐

d) Would he have laid hands on you? I don't think so. ☐

e) The police laid a trap to catch the thief. ☐

f) The police layd a trap to catch the thief. ☐

165 **Idioms - do you know their meaning? / Redewendungen - kennen Sie ihre Bedeutung?**

a) to lay the table ______________________________

b) to lay one's cards on the table ______________________________

c) to lay stress on s.th. ______________________________

d) to lay claim on s.th. ______________________________

e) to lay it on a bit thick ______________________________

f) to lay the blame for s.th. on s.o. ______________________________

g) to lay hands on s.th. ______________________________

h) to lay plans ______________________________

lead

166 **Fill in the right form of the verb: / Setzen Sie die korrekte Verbform ein:**

a) This blind man has a dog to ________ him.

b) The group was ________ through the whole country by a travel guide.

c) A star had ________ the shepherds to the stable.

167 **Cross out the wrong forms: / Streichen Sie die falschen Verbformen durch:**

a) This teacher lead/leads her class quite well.

b) I'm sure she lead/led a double life in her youth.

c) Please, lead/led me out of this labyrinth of streets.

Idioms - do you know their meaning? / Redewendungen - kennen Sie ihre Bedeutung? 168

a) to lead the way ______________________

b) to lead s.o. astray ______________________

c) to lead s.o. on ______________________

d) to lead s.o. up the garden path ______________________

e) to lead s.o. by the nose ______________________

f) to lead up to ______________________

leap

Fill in the right form of the verb: / Setzen Sie die korrekte Verbform ein: 169

a) Horses ________ over a fence without difficulty. (pres.)

b) When she heard the news she ________ out of her chair.

c) As fast as he had ________ into the cold water, he hastened to get out of it again.

Which is the correct sentence? / Welcher Satz ist richtig? 170

a) He went two steps back and then he leaped over the hedge as if it was nothing. ☐

b) He went two steps back and then he lept over the hedge as if it was nothing. ☐

c) He was scared that the big dog would leaps over the fence as well. ☐

d) He was scared that the big dog would leap over the fence as well. ☐

Idioms - do you know their meaning? / Redewendungen - kennen Sie ihre Bedeutung? 171

a) to leap at a chance ______________________

b) to leap at an offer ______________________

c) to leap out at s.o. ______________________

d) to leap into s.o.'s mind ______________________

e) Look before you leap! ______________________________

f) to make hearts leap for joy ______________________________

learn

172 **Fill in the right form of the verb: / Setzen Sie die korrekte Verbform ein:**

a) Schools are places where children are supposed to _______ important things for their lives.

b) As soon as we _______ of his illness we went to visit him.

c) I am glad that I have _______ English.

173 **Cross out the wrong forms: / Streichen Sie die falschen Verbformen durch:**

a) How did you learn/learned to speak English so well?

b) My dog has learned/learnt/learnet to run before a sledge.

c) Most children learned/learnt/learnet from experience whatever they know of the world.

174 **Idioms - do you know their meaning? / Redewendungen - kennen Sie ihre Bedeutung?**

a) to learn s.th. by heart ______________________________

b) to learn s.th. the hard way ______________________________

c) to learn one's lesson ______________________________

d) you live and learn ______________________________

leave

175 **Fill in the right form of the verb: / Setzen Sie die korrekte Verbform ein:**

a) _______ the door open, please, Mum has just come home.

b) He _______ all his belongings in her room. (s.p.)

c) My uncle had ________ by car and came back on foot. Can you imagine what had happened?

Form meaningful sentences: / Bilden Sie sinnvolle Sätze: 176

a) If he	left	me I'll never be the same.
b) Her friends had	leaves	my backpack in the train.
c) I	left	the pub before she arrived.

Idioms - do you know their meaning? / Redewendungen - kennen Sie ihre Bedeutung? 177

a) to leave no stone unturned ________________________

b) to leave s.o. alone ________________________

c) to leave a lot to be desired ________________________

d) to leave s.o. in the lurch ________________________

e) to leave s.o. cold ________________________

f) to leave s.th. at that ________________________

g) to leave s.th. to chance ________________________

h) to be left out in the cold ________________________

i) to be left (over) ________________________

j) to leave for Edinburgh ________________________

k) to be left until called for ________________________

lend

Fill in the right form of the verb: / Setzen Sie die korrekte Verbform ein: 178

a) I will ________ you the car if you promise to drive carefully.

b) She ________ me her coat because it was very cold.

c) I have ________ all my good books to a good friend.

Which is the correct sentence? / Welcher Satz ist richtig? 179

a) Lend me your ear and I'll sing you a song. ☐

b) Lent me your ear and I'll sing you a song. ☐

c) Our grass had to be cut so a friend lent a lawnmower to us. ☐

d) Our grass had to be cut so a friend lend a lawnmower to us. ☐

e) It's raining cats and dogs. Could you lent me your umbrella? ☐

f) It's raining cats and dogs. Could you lend me your umbrella? ☐

180 Idioms - do you know their meaning? / Redewendungen - kennen Sie ihre Bedeutung?

a) to lend one's aid ______________________

b) to lend s.o. a hand with s.th. ______________________

He used *to lend his father a hand with the gardening*.

c) to lend oneself to s.th. ______________________

d) to lend itself to s.th. ______________________

e) to lend an ear to s.o. ______________________

let

181 Fill in the right form of the verb: / Setzen Sie die korrekte Verbform ein:

a) Please, Mum, ________ me go out tonight.

b) They always ________ her do what she wanted.

c) Why have you ________ him see the letter?

182 Cross out the wrong forms: / Streichen Sie die falschen Verbformen durch:

a) Let/Let's him go. He didn't do any harm.

b) She never lets/let anyone look into the pots when she is cooking.

c) After having asked him numerous questions they finally let/led him go.

183 Idioms - do you know their meaning? / Redewendungen - kennen Sie ihre Bedeutung?

a) to let a room ______________________

b) to let the cat out of the bag ______________________

c) let alone ______________________

d) to let drop a remark ______________________________

e) to let off steam ______________________________

f) to let oneself go ______________________________

g) to let oneself in on s.th. ______________________________

h) to let one's hair down ______________________________

i) to let go of s.th. ______________________________

j) to let s.o. down ______________________________

k) to let s.o. into a secret ______________________________

l) to let s.o. off ______________________________

m) to let s.th. slip ______________________________

n) to let on that... ______________________________

o) let me see... ______________________________

lie

Fill in the right form of the verb: / Setzen Sie die korrekte Verbform ein: 184

a) Bonn _______ behind the hills. (pres.)

b) Grandmother _______ in bed for a week but now she is up again.

c) She has _______ herself down as if she were never to get up again.

Which is the correct sentence? / Welcher Satz ist richtig? 185

a) She was so tired that all she wanted was to lie down and sleep. ☐

b) She was so tired that all she wanted was to lay down and sleep. ☐

c) The house lay in a very quiet street. ☐

d) The house lied in a very quiet street. ☐

Idioms - do you know their meaning? / Redewendungen - kennen Sie ihre Bedeutung? 186

a) it lies with you ______________________________

b) to lie heavily on s.o. ______________________________

c) to lie in ______________________________

d) to lie back in an armchair ______________________________

e) to lie in ruins ______________________

f) to lie low ______________________

g) to lie under an obligation ______________________

h) to lie in store for s.o. ______________________

i) Let sleeping dogs lie. ______________________

j) to see how the land lies ______________________

k) to know where one's interest lies ______________________

light

187 **Fill in the right form of the verb: / Setzen Sie die korrekte Verbform ein:**

a) David ________ the candles before they sit down to dinner every evening.

b) We ________ a huge fire because it was very cold.

c) Look, he has just ________ another cigarette.

188 **Which is the correct sentence? / Welcher Satz ist richtig?**

a) With my torch I lit up the whole room. ☐

b) With my torch I lighted up the whole room. ☐

c) With my torch I lid up the whole room. ☐

d) Shall I lit your cigarette for you? ☐

e) Shall I light your cigarette for you? ☐

189 **Idioms - do you know their meaning? / Redewendungen - kennen Sie ihre Bedeutung?**

a) to light upon s.th. ______________________

b) to be lit up ______________________

After three beer he is usually *lit up*.

c) to throw a new light on s.th. ______________________

lose

Fill in the right form of the verb: / Setzen Sie die korrekte Verbform ein: 190

a) No matter how often we play with each other, I always _______.

b) In all this chaos I even _______ my car keys. (s.p.)

c) He has _______ his patience again. Can you hear him shouting?

Form meaningful sentences: / Bilden Sie sinnvolle Sätze: 191

a) She was angry for	lose	him continually in the crowd.
b) She will	losing	my patience as quickly as yesterday.
c) I have never	lost	every single bet. It's not her lucky day.

Idioms - do you know their meaning? / Redewendungen - kennen Sie ihre Bedeutung? 192

a) to lose one's head ______________________________

b) to lose the thread (of one's argument) ______________________________

c) to lose much sleep over/about s.th. ______________________________

d) to lose one's mind ______________________________

e) to lose one's temper ______________________________

f) to lose heart ______________________________

g) to lose one's heart to s.th./s.o. ______________________________

h) to lose sight of s.th. ______________________________

i) to lose track of s.th. ______________________________

j) to lose touch with s.o. ______________________________

k) to lose one's way ______________________________

l) to be lost in thought ______________________________

make

193 **Fill in the right form of the verb: / Setzen Sie die korrekte Verbform ein:**

a) Let's ________ a cake for grandfather's birthday.

b) It ________ me happy to see them talking together. (s.p.)

c) She has ________ this coat herself.

194 **Cross out the wrong forms: / Streichen Sie die falschen Verbformen durch:**

a) He has never maked/made a cake in his life.

b) Don't make/makes such a fuss.

c) This alarm-clock is "Made/Maked in Germany" and it's broken already.

195 **Idioms - do you know their meaning? / Redewendungen - kennen Sie ihre Bedeutung?**

a) to make s.o. do s.th. ________________________________

b) to make both ends meet ________________________________

c) to make a deal with s.o. ________________________________

d) to make a fuss about s.th. ________________________________

e) to make a mountain out of a molehill ________________________

f) to make eyes at s.o. ________________________________

g) to make do with s.th. ________________________________

h) to make friends with s.o. ________________________________

i) to make up for s.th. ________________________________

j) to make it ________________________________

k) to make the best of it ________________________________

l) to make the most of it ________________________________

m) to make up one's mind ________________________________

n) to be unable to make head or tail of s.th. ____________________

o) to make s.o.'s hair stand on end ____________________________

p) to make a point of s.th. ________________________________

q) to make for the door ________________________________

r) Make yourself at home! ____________________________

s) to make sense of s.th. ____________________________

mean

Fill in the right form of the verb: / Setzen Sie die korrekte Verbform ein: 196

a) I never know what he _______.

b) There were no tickets left. It _______ that they had to go home again.

c) Peter has always _______ a lot to me so I keep on writing to him.

Which is the correct sentence? / Welcher Satz ist richtig? 197

a) He meaned to do her no harm but she was frightened, nevertheless. ☐

b) He meant to do her no harm but she was frightened, nevertheless. ☐

c) Do you know what this sign means? ☐

d) Do you know what this sign mean? ☐

Idioms - do you know their meaning? / Redewendungen - kennen Sie ihre Bedeutung? 198

a) to mean to do s.th. ____________________________

b) to mean well ____________________________

c) not mean harm ____________________________

d) to mean business ____________________________

meet

Fill in the right form of the verb: / Setzen Sie die korrekte Verbform ein: 199

a) Everytime I go shopping I _______ someone I know.

b) Driving further they saw that the two roads _______ in the distance.

c) We couldn't believe that we had _______ them in the middle of nowhere.

200 **Form meaningful sentences: / Bilden Sie sinnvolle Sätze:**

a) We will be	met	him again.
b) I want to	meeting	the landlord tomorrow at 8 o'clock.
c) The boy	meet	his friends every day after school.

201 **Idioms - do you know their meaning? / Redewendungen - kennen Sie ihre Bedeutung?**

a) to meet a difficulty ______________________________

b) to meet s.o.'s expectations ______________________________

c) to meet with an accident ______________________________

d) to meet with success ______________________________

e) to meet with approval ______________________________

f) to meet with a refusal ______________________________

g) to meet one's fate ______________________________

h) to meet one's end ______________________________

i) to meet s.o.'s eye ______________________________

j) to meet up with s.o. ______________________________

pay

202 **Fill in the right form of the verb: / Setzen Sie die korrekte Verbform ein:**

a) I do hope they will ________ their rent punctually.

b) They ________ and left the restaurant.

c) He hasn't ________ one of the ten bills yet.

203 **Which is the correct sentence? / Welcher Satz ist richtig?**

a) The couple couldn't pay the rent anymore. They had to move. ☐

b) The couple couldn't paid the rent anymore. They had to move. ☐

c) I payt for the old table with a cheque. ☐

d) I paid for the old table with a cheque. ☐

Idioms - do you know their meaning? / Redewendungen - kennen Sie ihre Bedeutung? 204

a) to pay attention to s.th./s.o. ______________________

b) to pay heed to s.th./s.o. ______________________

c) to pay s.o. back ______________________

d) to pay s.o. a visit ______________________

e) to pay s.o. a compliment ______________________

f) to pay homage to s.o. ______________________

g) to pay through the nose for s.th. (coll.) ______________________

h) to pay one's way ______________________

i) to pay dearly for s.th. ______________________

j) to pay off ______________________

k) to pay for itself ______________________

put

Fill in the right form of the verb: / Setzen Sie die korrekte Verbform ein: 205

a) We usually ________ seven plates on the table. One for each of us six and one for Harvey. (pres.)

b) Jenny ________ her books away. (s.p.)

c) I have ________ the clothes in the cupboard.

Cross out the wrong forms: / Streichen Sie die falschen Verbformen durch: 206

a) She has putted/put all her belongings into boxes.

b) The children have put/pud a lot of water into their sandpit.

c) Please, put/puts your suitcase in the guestroom.

Idioms - do you know their meaning? / Redewendungen - kennen Sie ihre Bedeutung? 207

a) to put an end to s.th. ______________________

b) to put s.o. in his place ______________________

c) to put into words ______________________________

d) to put on weight ______________________________

e) to put one's foot in it ______________________________

f) to put one's foot down ______________________________

g) to put the lid on s.th. ______________________________

h) to put the screws on s.o. ______________________________

i) to put s.th. right ______________________________

j) to put s.o. up ______________________________

k) to put the blame for s.th. on s.o. ______________________________

l) to put the cart before the horse ______________________________

m) to put up with s.th. ______________________________

n) to put a spoke in s.o.'s wheel ______________________________

o) to put in an appearance ______________________________

p) not put it past s.o. ______________________________

q) to put one's mind to s.th. ______________________________

r) to put into action/practice ______________________________

s) to put s.o. to shame ______________________________

t) to put s.th. off ______________________________

u) to be put off by s.th. ______________________________

v) to put on an act ______________________________

read

208 **Fill in the right form of the verb: / Setzen Sie die korrekte Verbform ein:**

a) My friend likes to ________ the newspaper while he eats his breakfast.

b) I was so embarrassed because he ________ the letter out loud.

c) This morning I have ________ a lot about teaching classes.

209 **Cross out the wrong forms: / Streichen Sie die falschen Verbformen:**

a) I readed/read about their wedding in the local paper.

b) How many books can you reads/read in a week?

c) He has read/reads all the books by Charles Dickens.

d) We like to reat/read a story to our children before they go to bed.

Idioms - do you know their meaning? / Redewendungen - kennen Sie ihre Bedeutung? 210

a) to read between the lines ______________________

b) to read s.o. like a book ______________________

c) to read a subject at University ______________________

d) to read on ______________________

e) to read s.th. out ______________________

f) to read up on s.th. ______________________

g) to take it as read that... ______________________

h) to be well-read in s.th. ______________________

ride

Fill in the right form of the verb: / Setzen Sie die korrekte Verbform ein: 211

a) The cowboy ________ on his horse through the prairie every day. (pres.)

b) He ________ his bicycle to school when he was only ten years old.

c) Have you ever ________ on a camel?

Form meaningful sentences: / Bilden Sie sinnvolle Sätze: 212

a) To	rode	in years. I must have forgotten everything.
b) Grandfather	ridden	an elephant you must go to India.
c) I haven't	ride	his pony to school when he was young.

Idioms - do you know their meaning? / Redewendungen - kennen Sie ihre Bedeutung? 213

a) to ride one's hobby-horse ______________________

b) to ride again ______________________

c) to ride on air ______________________________

d) to ride for a fall ______________________________

e) to ride high ______________________________

f) to let s.th. ride ______________________________

g) to ride roughshot over s.th. ______________________________

h) to be ridden by fears ______________________________

rise

214 **Fill in the right form of the verb: / Setzen Sie die korrekte Verbform ein:**

a) How beautiful the sky looks when the sun is about to ________.

b) Even during our holidays we ________ very early in the morning.

c) Prices for chocolates have not ________ for years.

215 **Form meaningful sentences: / Bilden Sie sinnvolle Sätze:**

a) The horse tried to	rise	and I believe it's a full moon tonight.
b) We both	risen	but with it's broken leg it couldn't manage.
c) The moon has	rose	at once and ran into the garden.

216 **Idioms - do you know their meaning? / Redewendungen - kennen Sie ihre Bedeutung?**

a) to rise to the occasion ______________________________

b) to rise (up) against s.o. ______________________________

c) to rise from the dead ______________________________

d) Christ is risen! ______________________________

e) Rise and shine! ______________________________

f) to rise above s.th. ______________________________

g) to rise in society ______________________________

run

Fill in the right form of the verb: / Setzen Sie die korrekte Verbform ein: 217

a) She _______ three miles in fifteen minutes. (pres.)

b) The thief _______ away with the stolen money. (s.p.)

c) The policeman had _______ as fast as he could and finally caught the robber.

Cross out the wrong forms: / Streichen Sie die falschen Verbformen durch: 218

a) He will always runs/run faster than you.

b) I dreamed that I ran/run and ran/run and never reached the house.

c) When he saw her he runs/ran as fast as he could to meet her.

Idioms - do you know their meaning? / Redewendungen - kennen Sie ihre Bedeutung? 219

a) to run across s.o. ____________________

b) to run ashore ____________________

c) to run a business ____________________

d) to run errands ____________________

e) to run the household ____________________

f) to run the show ____________________

g) to run for Presidency ____________________

h) to run out of s.th. ____________________

i) to run short of s.th. ____________________

j) to run s.o. over ____________________

k) to run high ____________________

l) to run a temperature ____________________

m) it runs in the family ____________________

n) to run dry ____________________

o) to run a risk ____________________

p) to run into debt ____________________

q) to run into trouble ____________________

r) to run for one's life ____________________

s) to run a race ____________________

t) to run the streets ____________________

u) still waters run deep ____________________

say

220 **Fill in the right form of the verb: / Setzen Sie die korrekte Verbform ein:**

a) You must _______ the truth.

b) He _______ something very rude on the phone yesterday.

c) We couldn't remember what he had _______.

221 **Which is the correct sentence? / Welcher Satz ist richtig?**

a) I wonder what he'll says when he hears the news. ☐

b) I wonder what he'll say when he hears the news. ☐

c) Has she said anything nice about me? ☐

d) Has she sayed anything nice about me? ☐

e) How do you said "I love you" in Spanish? ☐

f) How do you say "I love you" in Spanish? ☐

222 **Idioms - do you know their meaning? / Redewendungen - kennen Sie ihre Bedeutung?**

a) no sooner said than done ____________________

b) that is easier said than done ____________________

c) it goes without saying that ____________________

d) You don't say! ____________________

e) You can say that again! ____________________

f) and that's saying something ____________________

g) that is to say, . . . ____________________

h) let's say ____________________

i) to say nothing of . . . ____________________

j) when all is said and done ___________________________

k) not be able to say boo to a goose ___________________________

l) to say grace ___________________________

m) to say to oneself ___________________________

see

Fill in the right form of the verb: / Setzen Sie die korrekte Verbform ein: 223

a) Will you come to _______ me tomorrow?

b) Yesterday I _______ this man climbing up a wall.

c) I have _______ many colourful butterflies this summer.

Form meaningful sentences: / Bilden Sie sinnvolle Sätze: 224

a) From the top of the tree I	seen	anything at all?
b) I have	see	the village in the distance.
c) With that mass of hair can you	saw	him twice today.

Idioms - do you know their meaning? / Redewendungen - kennen Sie ihre Bedeutung? 225

a) to see no further than one's nose ___________________________

b) to see to s.th. ___________________________

c) to see the back/last of s.o. ___________________________

d) to see eye to eye with s.o. ___________________________

e) to see for oneself ___________________________

f) to see the light ___________________________

g) to see how the wind blows ___________________________

h) to see s.o. home ___________________________

i) to see s.o. off ___________________________

j) to see s.o. out ___________________________

k) to have seen better days ___________________________

l) to see s.o.'s point ___________________________

m) to see s.th. through ___________________________

n) to see s.o. through s.th. ____________________

o) to see to it that . . . ____________________

p) to see red ____________________

q) not to see the wood for the trees ____________________

r) Seeing is believing! ____________________

s) to live to see s.th. ____________________

seek

226 **Fill in the right form of the verb: / Setzen Sie die korrekte Verbform ein:**

a) It's too cold in the shade. Let's ________ a sunny place.

b) She did not know what to do, so she ________ her advice.

c) Mum has ________ to convince me several times.

227 **Which is the correct sentence? / Welcher Satz ist richtig?**

a) I'll never stop to seeks the meaning in life. ☐

b) I'll never stop to seek the meaning in life. ☐

c) She sought my help whenever she was in trouble. ☐

d) She seeked my help whenever she was in trouble. ☐

228 **Idioms - do you know their meaning? / Redewendungen - kennen Sie ihre Bedeutung?**

a) to seek one's fortune ____________________

b) to seek s.o.'s life ____________________

c) to seek s.o. out ____________________

d) to be much sought-after ____________________

The president is so *much sought-after* that she never gets a moment's rest.

sell

Fill in the right form of the verb: / Setzen Sie die korrekte Verbform ein: 229

a) In our shop we also ________ fish and chips. (pres.)

b) Grandfather ________ his old piano for a lot of money. (s.p.)

c) I would have ________ my computer long ago but no one wanted it.

Cross out the wrong forms: / Streichen Sie die falschen Verbformen durch: 230

a) They have sold/seld all the cheap jeans already.

b) The boy is sells/selling all sorts of strange articles.

c) We couldn't get any tickets because the performance was selled/sold out.

Idioms - do you know their meaning? / Redewendungen - kennen Sie ihre Bedeutung? 231

a) to sell s.o. down the river ________________________________

b) to be sold on s.th. ________________________________

c) to be sold ________________________________

d) to sell at a loss ________________________________

e) to sell like hot cakes ________________________________

send

Fill in the right form of the verb: / Setzen Sie die korrekte Verbform ein: 232

a) I'd like to ________ an invitation to all my good friends.

b) He ________ her away as he didn't want to see her anymore.

c) These children have been ________ to boarding school by their parents.

Which is the correct sentence? / Welcher Satz ist richtig? 233

a) Don't send me away, yet. I'd like to stay a little longer. ☐

b) Don't sent me away, yet. I'd like to stay a little longer. ☐

c) I can't come to the party but I'll sent you a present. ☐

d) I can't come to the party but I'll send you a present. ☐

e) The last time I have send a letter to him is quite a while ago. ☐

f) The last time I sent a letter to him is quite a while ago. ☐

234 **Idioms - do you know their meaning? / Redewendungen - kennen Sie ihre Bedeutung?**

a) to send s.o. packing ______________________

b) to send s.o. flying ______________________

c) to send word to s.o. ______________________

d) to send a letter on to ______________________

set

235 **Fill in the right form of the verb: / Setzen Sie die korrekte Verbform ein:**

a) ________ the box down in the hall, please.

b) I ________ the magazine aside when the children came home.

c) They have ________ up the new dish-washer.

236 **Which is the correct sentence? / Welcher Satz ist richtig?**

a) Mary set her cup down and started to laugh helplessly. ☐

b) Mary setted her cup down and started to laugh helplessly. ☐

c) Her mind was set on winning. She would succeed, she knew it. ☐

d) Her mind was sat on winning. She would succeed, she knew it. ☐

237 **Idioms - do you know their meaning? / Redewendungen - kennen Sie ihre Bedeutung?**

a) to set s.o. free ______________________

b) to set out for ______________________

c) to set out on a journey ______________________

d) to set out to do s.th. ______________________

e) to set about doing s.th. ______________________________

f) to set eyes on s.th. ______________________________

g) to set fire to s.th. ______________________________

h) to set s.th. on fire ______________________________

i) to set foot in ______________________________

j) to set the alarm-clock ______________________________

k) to set in ______________________________

l) to set people at loggerheads ______________________________

m) to set one's mind on s.th. ______________________________

n) to set one's mind at rest ______________________________

o) to be all set for s.th. ______________________________

p) to set the fashion ______________________________

q) to set the pace ______________________________

r) to be dead set against s.th. ______________________________

s) to set one's heart on s.th. ______________________________

t) to be set on doing s.th. ______________________________

u) to set a good example ______________________________

v) to set s.o.'s teeth on edge ______________________________

w) to set a poem to music ______________________________

x) to set the table ______________________________

shake

Fill in the right form of the verb: / Setzen Sie die korrekte Verbform ein: 238

a) The earth is ________. This must be an earthquake.

b) I ________ all the rugs this morning. (s.p.)

c) Instead of an answer he had only ________ his head.

Form meaningful sentences: / Bilden Sie sinnvolle Sätze: 239

a) It says you have to	shaken	the juice before opening it.
b) Her whole body still	shake	off the police.
c) I think we have	shook	with fear.

240 **Idioms - do you know their meaning? / Redewendungen - kennen Sie ihre Bedeutung?**

a) to shake hands with s.o. ______

b) to shake the dust of a place off one's feet ______

c) to shake one's fist at s.o. ______

d) to shake like a leaf ______

e) to shake in one's shoes ______

f) to be shaken by s.th. ______

g) to shake s.o. up ______

h) to shake s.o.'s faith ______

i) Shake a leg! ______

shed

241 **Fill in the right form of the verb: / Setzen Sie die korrekte Verbform ein:**

a) The boys always ______ their clothes before they jump into the lake. (pres.)

b) When she heard of his death she ______ many tears.

c) They told us that we had ______ our blood for the country.

242 **Cross out the wrong forms: / Streichen Sie die falschen Verbformen durch:**

a) Snakes shed/shet their skin once a year.

b) The oven shed/sheded a very pleasant warmth.

243 **Idioms - do you know their meaning? / Redewendungen - kennen Sie ihre Bedeutung?**

a) to shed light on s.th. ______

b) to shed it's skin ______

c) to shed their leaves ______

d) to shed a bad habit ______

e) to shed a few pounds ______

f) to shed one's inhibitions ______________________________

g) not to shed a tear over s.o. ______________________________

shine

Fill in the right form of the verb: / Setzen Sie die korrekte Verbform ein: 244

a) Draw the lamp a little closer, please, so that it _______ on my book. (fut.)

b) Her beautiful hair _______ in the sun. (s.p.)

c) On their wedding day his eyes had _______ with happiness.

Cross out the wrong forms: / Streichen Sie die falschen Verbformen durch: 245

a) Tomorrow, the sun will shine/shone again.

b) Jack polished his car until it shined/shone.

c) The light in his room is shining/shown, he must be home.

Idioms - do you know their meaning? / Redewendungen - kennen Sie ihre Bedeutung? 246

a) Rise and shine! ______________________________

b) to shine in/at s.th. ______________________________

c) to shine a lamp on s.th. ______________________________

d) to shine up to someone (AE) ______________________________

shoot

Fill in the right form of the verb: / Setzen Sie die korrekte Verbform ein: 247

a) Every time he _______ his arrows miss the target.

b) The politician was _______ by a fanatic.

c) Many people have been _______ in the war.

248 **Which is the correct sentence? / Welcher Satz ist richtig?**

a) Being in a great hurry, he shot out of the house. ☐

b) Being in a great hurry, he shoot out of the house. ☐

c) In Africa people still shooted big game. ☐

d) In Africa people still shoot big game. ☐

249 **Idioms - do you know their meaning? / Redewendungen - kennen Sie ihre Bedeutung?**

a) a shot in the dark ________________

b) to shoot ahead ________________

c) to have shot one's bolt ________________

d) to shoot questions at s.o. ________________

e) to shoot the lights ________________

f) to shoot a glance at s.th. ________________

g) to shoot a film ________________

h) to shoot heroin ________________

show

250 **Fill in the right form of the verb: / Setzen Sie die korrekte Verbform ein:**

a) Dogs ________ their teeth when they are angry or frightened.

b) She ________ me the way when I was lost.

c) At the border she had ________ her passport to almost every official.

251 **Form meaningful sentences: / Bilden Sie sinnvolle Sätze:**

a) Jenny has	shown	all my photographs at the meeting.
b) I will	showed	you how to milk the cows, hasn't she?
c) They	show	us what they thought quite clearly.

252 **Idioms - do you know their meaning? / Redewendungen - kennen Sie ihre Bedeutung?**

a) to show s.o. in ________________

b) to show s.o. out ____________________

c) to show off with s.th. ____________________

d) to show s.o. round ____________________

e) to show up ____________________

f) to show one's hand/cards ____________________

g) to show s.o. around the town ____________________

h) to show one's teeth ____________________

shrink

Fill in the right form of the verb: / Setzen Sie die korrekte Verbform ein: 253

a) My pullovers usually ________ with each washing. (pres.)

b) The number of guests ________ rapidly after 12 o'clock. (s.p.)

c) The mushrooms have ________ a lot in the frying pan.

Form meaningful sentences: / Bilden Sie sinnvolle Sätze: 254

a) They seem to	shrank	back from her daily tasks.
b) Sue	shrink	ten centimetres. I will make a complaint.
c) My new blanket has	shrunk	into themselves when he shouts.

Idioms - do you know their meaning? / Redewendungen - kennen Sie ihre Bedeutung? 255

a) to shrink (back) from s.th. ____________________

b) to shrink into oneself ____________________

When lost in thought she always seemed *to shrink into herself.*

shut

Fill in the right form of the verb: / Setzen Sie die korrekte Verbform ein: 256

a) Now ________ your eyes and go to sleep.

b) I didn't want to see that part of the film so I ________ my eyes.

c) I have ________ all the windows to keep out the rain.

257 **Cross out the wrong forms: / Streichen Sie die falschen Verbformen durch:**

a) Shut/Shuts your mouth when your are eating!

b) The door banged shut/shud.

c) I'm sure they have shuted/shut the windows properly.

258 **Idioms - do you know their meaning? / Redewendungen - kennen Sie ihre Bedeutung?**

a) Shut up! (coll.) ________________________________

b) to shut s.o. up ________________________________

c) to shut s.th.down ________________________________

d) to shut s.th.off ________________________________

e) to be shut off from s.th. ________________________________

f) to shut one's eyes to s.th. ________________________________

g) to keep one's mouth shut ________________________________

h) to shut oneself in ________________________________

sing

259 **Fill in the right form of the verb: / Setzen Sie die korrekte Verbform ein:**

a) She has got a beautiful voice and ________ a lot. (pres.)

b) For one concert they ________ together. (s.p.)

c) Grandmother had ________ us a song before we went to bed.

260 **Form meaningful sentences: / Bilden Sie sinnvolle Sätze:**

a) The birds have	sing	all day long. Spring must be coming.
b) Two people	sung	me a song? I'd like to hear your voice.
c) Would you	sang	completely out of tune.

Idioms - do you know their meaning? / Redewendungen - kennen Sie ihre Bedeutung? 261

a) to sing another song/tune ______
b) to sing the same song/tune ______
c) to sing s.o. to sleep ______
d) to sing small/low ______
e) to sing s.o.'s praises ______
f) to sing out ______
g) to sing up ______
h) to sing of s.th./s.o. ______
i) to sing one's heart out ______

sink

Fill in the right form of the verb: / Setzen Sie die korrekte Verbform ein: 262

a) Our boat cannot ______.
b) When the boat got a hole it ______ quickly.
c) Fortunately, prices have ______ again.

Form meaningful sentences: / Bilden Sie sinnvolle Sätze: 263

a) Relieved, she	sinking	into her chair exhaustedly.
b) I believe the ship is	sunk	into their arms.
c) Linda had	sank	fast.

Idioms - do you know their meaning? / Redewendungen - kennen Sie ihre Bedeutung? 264

a) to sink into oblivion ______
b) to sink into sleep ______
c) to sink into grief ______
d) sink or swim ______
e) s.o.'s heart sinks into one's boots ______

sit

265 Fill in the right form of the verb: / Setzen Sie die korrekte Verbform ein:

a) I'll ________ on this chair instead of the other one. I think it's more comfortable.

b) The youngsters ________ on that bench every night last week.

c) We have ________ in the first row in the cinema. Now we both have stiff necks.

266 Which is the correct sentence? / Welcher Satz ist richtig?

a) Don't just sit around. Come and dance with me. ☐

b) Don't just sits around. Come and dance with me. ☐

c) We sitted at the table and waited for the food to come. ☐

d) We sat at the table and waited for the food to come. ☐

267 Idioms - do you know their meaning? / Redewendungen - kennen Sie ihre Bedeutung?

a) to sit back and do nothing ________________

b) to sit on one's hands ________________

c) to sit in ________________

d) to sit for an exam ________________

e) to sit on the fence ________________

f) to sit up for s.o. ________________

g) to sit tight ________________

h) to sit up and take notice ________________

i) to be sitting pretty ________________

j) to sit to s.o. ________________

k) Sit up straight! ________________

sleep

Fill in the right form of the verb: / Setzen Sie die korrekte Verbform ein: 268

a) On weekends she ________ as long as she likes.

b) I dreamt a lot and ________ very restless.

c) They had ________ in the cave for weeks before someone found them.

Cross out the wrong forms: / Streichen Sie die falschen Verbformen durch: 269

a) I long to be able to sleep/slept as long as I like.

b) Peter sleeped/slept in today and missed the bus.

c) Have you slept/sleeped at all last night?

Idioms - do you know their meaning? / Redewendungen - kennen Sie ihre Bedeutung? 270

a) to sleep (s.th.) away ________________________________

b) to sleep through s.th. ________________________________

c) to sleep in ________________________________

d) to sleep like a log ________________________________

e) to sleep the sleep of the just ________________________________

f) to sleep on/over a problem ________________________________

g) I must sleep on it first ________________________________

h) to sleep off one's lunch ________________________________

i) to sleep off a hangover ________________________________

j) to sleep with s.o. ________________________________

slide

Which is the correct sentence? / Welcher Satz ist richtig? 271

a) The slope was so steep we couldn't help sliding down. ☐

b) The slope was so steep we couldn't help slide down. ☐

c) She loves to slid on ice, so when the lake was frozen she put on her slippery shoes and slided for an hour. ☐

d) She loves to slide on ice, so when the lake was frozen she put on her slippery shoes and slid for an hour. ☐

272 **Fill in the right form of the verb: / Setzen Sie die korrekte Verbform ein:**

a) He saw that he was watched so he let the parcel ________ back into his pocket.

b) The children ________ on the ice last winter.

c) Has he ________ out of the room unseen again?

273 **Idioms - do you know their meaning? / Redewendungen - kennen Sie ihre Bedeutung?**

a) to slide into s.th. ________________________________

b) to slide out of s.th. ________________________________

c) to let things slide ________________________________

d) to slide over s.th. ________________________________

Not wanting to answer my question, he slid over it elegantly.

____

smell

274 **Fill in the right form of the verb: / Setzen Sie die korrekte Verbform ein:**

a) I can ________ the spring.

b) He hadn't washed for days and ________ horrible.

c) She had ________ a field of roses for the first time in her life.

275 **Which is the correct sentence? / Welcher Satz ist richtig?**

a) Someone must have started to cook. It smelling good. ☐

b) Someone must have started to cook. It smells good. ☐

c) Hanna had smelt him coming because of his new aftershave. ☐

d) Hanna had smelled him coming because of his new aftershave. ☐

Idioms - do you know their meaning? / Redewendungen - kennen Sie ihre Bedeutung? 276

a) to smell about/around ______________________

b) to smell a rat ______________________

c) to smell fishy ______________________

d) to smell s.th. out ______________________

e) to smell trouble ______________________

speak

Fill in the right form of the verb: / Setzen Sie die korrekte Verbform ein: 277

a) Do you ________ English?

b) They ________ a lot of the conference, but nothing was new to me.

c) Have you ________ to him about this matter?

Form meaningful sentences: / Bilden Sie sinnvolle Sätze: 278

a) We haven't	spoken	to us about their travels in Asia.
b) He	speak	since our quarrel last week.
c) They will	spoke	to her in a low voice.

Idioms - do you know their meaning? / Redewendungen - kennen Sie ihre Bedeutung? 279

a) Actions speak louder than words. ______________________

b) speak of the devil ______________________

c) not to speak of ______________________

d) nothing to speak of ______________________

e) so to speak ______________________

f) to speak one's mind ______________________

g) to speak volumes ______________________

h) to speak well/ill of s.o. ______________________

i) not be on speaking terms with s.o. ______________________

spend

280 **Fill in the right form of the verb: / Setzen Sie die korrekte Verbform ein:**

a) We always _______ our holidays in Greece. (pres.)

b) My grandfather _______ all his savings on his grandchildren. (s.p.)

c) I have _______ a whole year in a foreign country.

281 **Cross out the wrong forms: / Streichen Sie die falschen Verbformen durch:**

a) This woman spend/spent half of her life in a foreign country.

b) You have spend/spent all your money already? I don't believe it.

c) Let's spent/spend some time together, shall we?

282 **Idioms - do you know their meaning? / Redewendungen - kennen Sie ihre Bedeutung?**

a) All my energies are spent. ______________________________

b) It's money well spent. ______________________________

c) to be spent up ______________________________

spread

283 **Fill in the right form of the verb: / Setzen Sie die korrekte Verbform ein:**

a) He must be cold. I will _______ a blanket over him.

b) She _______ all her belongings on the floor. (s.p.)

c) The news of their marriage has _______ fast.

284 **Which is the correct sentence? / Welcher Satz ist richtig?**

a) This weed has spreaded all over the place. ☐

b) This weed has spread all over the place. ☐

c) For our picnic we will spreat two blankets on the grass. ☐

d) For our picnic we will spread two blankets on the grass. ☐

Idioms - do you know their meaning? / Redewendungen - kennen Sie ihre Bedeutung? 285

a) to spread like wild fire ____________________

b) to spread one's wings ____________________

c) to spread oneself ____________________

spring

Fill in the right form of the verb: / Setzen Sie die korrekte Verbform ein: 286

a) This window doesn't stay shut. It always ________ open again. (pres.)

b) The girl ________ over the fence and tore her skirt.

c) She had ________ to my rescue but it hadn't been necessary.

Form meaningful sentences: / Bilden Sie sinnvolle Sätze: 287

a) The door	spring	from that cliff there.
b) Where did this rumour	sprang	from?
c) I have	sprung	open but no one was to be seen.

Idioms - do you know their meaning? / Redewendungen - kennen Sie ihre Bedeutung? 288

a) to spring to the eyes ____________________

b) to spring to one's feet ____________________

c) to spring to life ____________________

d) to spring from ____________________

e) to spring s.th. on s.o. ____________________

f) to spring up ____________________

stand

Fill in the right form of the verb: / Setzen Sie die korrekte Verbform ein: 289

a) Don't ________ in the corner. Come and join us!

b) He ________ at the meeting point and waited for an hour.

c) A small house has ________ at the edge of this cliff for centuries.

290 **Cross out the wrong forms: / Streichen Sie die falschen Verbformen durch:**

a) I can't see a thing if he stand/stands in front of me.

b) Look at the clouds! We stood/stand a good chance of getting some rain later.

c) All seats were taken, so she stood/stand during the whole journey.

291 **Idioms - do you know their meaning? / Redewendungen - kennen Sie ihre Bedeutung?**

a) his hair stands on edge ________________

b) to stand about/around ________________

c) to stand a good chance ________________

d) to stand by s.o. ________________

e) to stand firm ________________

f) to stand for s.th. ________________

g) to stand in for s.o. ________________

h) to stand up for s.o. ________________

i) to stand up to s.o. ________________

j) to stand up against s.o./s.th. ________________

k) to stand s.o. up ________________

l) to stand on ceremony ________________

m) to stand out from ________________

n) to stand pat on one's opinion ________________

o) to stand together ________________

p) to stand the racket ________________

q) to stand one's rights ________________

r) to stand s.o. a drink ________________

s) to stand or fall ________________

t) to stand well with s.o. ________________

u) to stand s.th. on its head ________________

v) to stand a test ______________________________

w) that stands out a mile ______________________________

x) it stands to reason that . . . ______________________________

y) and so it stands ______________________________

steal

Fill in the right form of the verb: / Setzen Sie die korrekte Verbform ein: 292

a) He ________ something every time he goes into a shop.

b) Someone ________ my bicycle and brought it back again.

c) The man was certain that his neighbour's son had ________ his axe.

Form meaningful sentences: / Bilden Sie sinnvolle Sätze: 293

a) Never try to	steal	all the jewellery out of the safe.
b) They have	stole	anything in her life.
c) She never	stolen	out of his presence. He'll always notice.

Idioms - do you know their meaning? / Redewendungen - kennen Sie ihre Bedeutung? 294

a) to steal away ______________________________

b) to steal s.o.'s thunder ______________________________

c) to steal a glance at s.o./s.th. ______________________________

d) to steal a march on s.o. ______________________________

e) to steal the show from s.o. ______________________________

f) pick and steal ______________________________

They never got any pocket-money, so it was *pick and steal* for them wherever they went.

____

____

stick

295 **Fill in the right form of the verb: / Setzen Sie die korrekte Verbform ein:**

a) _______ the flowers in this jar. I can't find a vase just now.

b) They _______ the broken pieces together again. (s.p.)

c) I have _______ a pin in my hand. It hurts.

296 **Cross out the wrong forms: / Streichen Sie die falschen Verbformen durch:**

a) I talked to her, but suddenly she sticked/stuck her tongue out at me.

b) The twins always stick/sticks together.

c) We were stuck/stucked with him and could hardly stand it.

297 **Idioms - do you know their meaning? / Redewendungen - kennen Sie ihre Bedeutung?**

a) to stick about _______________

b) to stick at nothing _______________

c) to stick at s.th. _______________

d) to stick by s.o. _______________

e) to be stuck _______________

f) to be stuck on s.o. _______________

g) to be stuck with s.o./s.th. _______________

h) to stick from/out of _______________

i) that sticks out a mile _______________

j) to stick s.th. out _______________

k) to stick out like a sore thumb _______________

l) to stick in one's mind _______________

m) to stick to the point _______________

n) to stick to s.o. like a bur _______________

o) to stick to one's principles _______________

p) to stick to the rules _______________

q) to stick one's neck out (coll.) _______________

r) to stick one's nose into s.th. ______________________________

s) Stick 'em up! (coll.) ______________________________

strike

Fill in the right form of the verb: / Setzen Sie die korrekte Verbform ein: 298

a) The clock ________ the hour. (pres.)

b) Suddenly it ________ me that they must have told him everything. (s.p.)

c) Grandmother has been ________ by a falling apple.

Which is the correct sentence? / Welcher Satz ist richtig? 299

a) That tree is all black. It must have been striked by lightning. ☐

b) That tree is all black. It must have been struck by lightning. ☐

c) Every quarter of the hour the church clock strike loudly. ☐

d) Every quarter of the hour the church clock strikes loudly. ☐

Idioms - do you know their meaning? / Redewendungen - kennen Sie ihre Bedeutung? 300

a) to strike a blow against s.o. ______________________________

b) to strike a bargain ______________________________

c) to strike a match ______________________________

d) to strike s.o.'s eye ______________________________

e) to strike it rich ______________________________

f) to strike at the root of s.th. ______________________________

g) to strike a happy medium ______________________________

h) to strike while the iron is hot ______________________________

i) to strike up a conversation ______________________________

j) Does that strike a chord? ______________________________

k) to strike the right note ______________________________

l) to strike a false note ______________________________

sweat

301 **Fill in the right form of the verb: / Setzen Sie die korrekte Verbform ein:**

a) My friend _______ a lot in hot weather. (pres.)

b) Four hours they _______ over the maths exercises without being able to solve them. (s.p.)

c) The little girl had _______ so much her mother had to change her shirt.

302 **Which is the correct sentence? / Welcher Satz ist richtig?**

a) How ever hard she worked, she never swead one drop. ☐

b) How ever hard she worked, she never sweat one drop. ☐

c) How ever hard she worked, she never sweated one drop. ☐

d) She made me sit there for one hour. I really had to sweats it out. ☐

e) She made me sit there for one hour. I really had to sweat it out. ☐

303 **Idioms - do you know their meaning? / Redewendungen - kennen Sie ihre Bedeutung?**

a) to sweat blood over s.th. ______________________________

b) to sweat it out ______________________________

c) to sweat s.o. ______________________________

d) to make s.o. sweat ______________________________

sweep

304 **Fill in the right form of the verb: / Setzen Sie die korrekte Verbform ein:**

a) The housekeeper _______ the stairs every morning. (pres.)

b) The heavy wind _______ all the leaves away, yesterday.

c) While he was looking on she was _______ away by the crowd.

Cross out the wrong forms: / Streichen Sie die falschen Verbformen durch: 305

a) This year our chimney has already been sweeped/swept twice.

b) You must swep/sweep the broken glass away before someone steps into it.

Idioms - do you know their meaning? / Redewendungen - kennen Sie ihre Bedeutung? 306

a) to sweep across one's mind ______________________

b) to sweep s.th. aside ______________________

c) to sweep s.o. off one's feet ______________________

d) to sweep s.th. away ______________________

e) to sweep away s.o.'s doubts ______________________

f) to sweep s.th. under the carpet ______________________

g) New brooms sweep clean. ______________________

swim

Fill in the right form of the verb: / Setzen Sie die korrekte Verbform ein: 307

a) Oil ________ on top of water.

b) Last year he ________ faster than me.

c) Look, Susan has ________ all the way to the island.

Form meaningful sentences: / Bilden Sie sinnvolle Sätze: 308

a) Some dogs like to	swim	the whole day, yesterday.
b) My brother already	swam	but ours doesn't at all.
c) We have	swum	like a fish at the age of four.

Idioms - do you know their meaning? / Redewendungen - kennen Sie ihre Bedeutung? 309

a) to swim with the tide/stream ______________________

b) to swim against the tide ______________________

c) to swim in money ______________________________

d) to swim before one's eyes ______________________________

take

310 **Fill in the right form of the verb: / Setzen Sie die korrekte Verbform ein:**

a) She ________ him out to dance every evening. (pres.)

b) He ________ off his clothes before he jumped into the water to rescue his dog.

c) Have you ________ his remark seriously? You shouldn't have!

311 **Form meaningful sentences: / Bilden Sie sinnvolle Sätze:**

a) Please,	take	three pills because she felt very sick.
b) Who has	took	me to a football match.
c) She	taken	my books? I need them now.

312 **Idioms - do you know their meaning? / Redewendungen - kennen Sie ihre Bedeutung?**

a) to be taken aback ______________________________

b) to be taken with s.th. ______________________________

c) to take after s.o. ______________________________

d) to take a break ______________________________

e) to take s.th. amiss ______________________________

f) to take s.th. at face value ______________________________

g) to take a chance ______________________________

h) to take a fancy to s.th. ______________________________

i) to take a liking to s.th. ______________________________

j) to take s.th. for granted ______________________________

k) to take heart ______________________________

l) to take s.th. to heart ______________________________

m) to take s.o. in ______________________________

n) to take a look at s.th. ______________________________

o) to take to one's heels ______________________

p) to take notes ______________________

q) to take notice of s.th. ______________________

r) to take offence at s.th. ______________________

s) to take place ______________________

t) to take one's leave ______________________

u) to take one's time ______________________

v) to take s.o. at one's word ______________________

w) to take s.o. for someone else ______________________

x) to take effect ______________________

y) Take it or leave it! ______________________

z) to be taken for a ride ______________________

aa) to take the wind out of s.o.'s sails ______________________

bb) to take to drinking ______________________

cc) to take turns with s.o. ______________________

dd) Take it from me! ______________________

ee) That takes the biscuit! ______________________

ff) Take it easy! ______________________

teach

Fill in the right form of the verb: / Setzen Sie die korrekte Verbform ein: 313

a) My mother ________ English in a grammar school. (pres.)

b) Grandfather ________ me how to play Badminton when I was ten years old.

c) Haven't you been ________ any good manners at all?

Which is the correct sentence? / Welcher Satz ist richtig? 314

a) He teached Spanish and Biology. ☐

b) He tought Spanish and Biology. ☐

c) I'd like to teach small children to read and write. ☐

d) I'd like to teaches small children to read and write. ☐

e) My teacher has tought me many useful things. ☐

f) My teacher has teached me many useful things. ☐

315 **Idioms - do you know their meaning? / Redewendungen - kennen Sie ihre Bedeutung?**

a) to teach s.o. a lesson ____________________

b) That'll teach you! ____________________

tell

316 **Fill in the right form of the verb: / Setzen Sie die korrekte Verbform ein:**

a) If you ________ me how you feel I might be able to help you.

b) Charles ________ me a number of new jokes on Saturday night. (s.p.)

c) She has been ________ to be home by ten o'clock. That's why she is leaving already.

317 **Cross out the wrong forms: / Streichen Sie die falschen Verbformen durch:**

a) Will you tells/tell me how to get to your place, please.

b) They never told/teld me anything. I had to find it out myself.

c) If you tell/tells him what I have just telled/told you I'll never speak a word to you again.

318 **Idioms - do you know their meaning? / Redewendungen - kennen Sie ihre Bedeutung?**

a) to tell the world ____________________

b) to tell s.o. off ____________________

c) to tell s.th. to s.o.'s face ____________________

d) to tell tales ____________________

e) it's hard to tell ____________________

f) you can never tell ____________________

g) You are telling me! ____________________

h) Tell me another! ______________________________

i) I can tell you that . . . ______________________________

think

Fill in the right form of the verb: / Setzen Sie die korrekte Verbform ein: 319

a) When we are not together I _______ of my boyfriend every day.

b) He _______ of telling her about his feelings but didn't have the courage to start.

c) We have _______ about moving into a flat together.

Which is the correct sentence? / Welcher Satz ist richtig? 320

a) What do you think you are doing? Stop it at once! ☐

b) What do you thought you are doing? Stop it at once! ☐

c) Certainly, he has thinked of everything. ☐

d) Certainly, he has thought of everything. ☐

e) When I was a child I never thought I'd grow up. ☐

f) When I was a child I never thinked I'd grow up. ☐

Idioms - do you know their meaning? / Redewendungen - kennen Sie ihre Bedeutung? 321

a) to think the better of s.th. ______________________________

b) to think fit to do s.th. ______________________________

c) to think s.th. over ______________________________

d) to think twice about s.th. ______________________________

e) now that I come to think of it ______________________________

f) I thought as much ______________________________

g) That's what you think! ______________________________

h) to think the world of s.o. ______________________________

i) to think highly of s.o. ______________________________

j) to think s.th. up ______________________________

throw

322 **Fill in the right form of the verb: / Setzen Sie die korrekte Verbform ein:**

a) _______ me a cushion, please. The wall in my back is cold.

b) She was so happy that she _______ her hat high into the air.

c) He had _______ all her letters into the fire after she had left him.

323 **Form meaningful sentences: / Bilden Sie sinnvolle Sätze:**

a) Yesterday, I	throw	myself onto the sofa.
b) Her father had	threw	her old jeans in the bin. She was furious.
c) The horse tried to	thrown	him but he stayed in the saddle.

324 **Idioms - do you know their meaning? / Redewendungen - kennen Sie ihre Bedeutung?**

a) to throw oneself at s.o. ______________________________

b) to throw s.th. back at s.o. ______________________________

c) to throw caution to the winds ______________________________

d) to throw a fit ______________________________

e) to throw one's heart into s.th. ______________________________

f) to throw s.th. in ______________________________

g) to throw oneself into s.th. ______________________________

h) to throw doubt on s.th. ______________________________

i) to throw light on s.th. ______________________________

j) to throw cold water on s.th. ______________________________

k) to throw in the towel ______________________________

l) to throw in the sponge ______________________________

m) to throw s.o. off ______________________________

n) to throw s.th. over ______________________________

o) to throw up ______________________________

p) to throw one's weight about ______________________________

q) That threw me! ______________________________

understand

Fill in the right form of the verb: / Setzen Sie die korrekte Verbform ein: 325

a) I don't _______ what you want to tell me. Try to explain yourself, please.

b) Jacky _______ him well even though her knowledge of his language was quite poor.

c) Finally; my father has _______ the question.

Cross out the wrong forms: / Streichen Sie die falschen Verbformen durch: 326

a) If you try, you'll understand/understood what I'm explaining.

b) I understood/understand what he wanted immediately – only, I didn't want to give it to him.

Idioms - do you know their meaning? / Redewendungen - kennen Sie ihre Bedeutung? 327

a) that is understood _______________________________

b) I understand that . . . _____________________________

c) What do you understand by this? ______________________

win

Fill in the right form of the verb: / Setzen Sie die korrekte Verbform ein: 328

a) Our horse will _______ this race. I know he will.

b) I don't know how I _______ Frankie's sympathy, but I obviously did.

c) Have you ever _______ anything in a competition?

Which is the correct sentence? / Welcher Satz ist richtig? 329

a) Who do you think will wins? ☐

b) Who do you think will win? ☐

c) My father was extremely proud when I won the first prize in the contest. ☐

d) My father was extremely proud when I winned the first prize in the contest. ☐

330 **Idioms - do you know their meaning? / Redewendungen - kennen Sie ihre Bedeutung?**

a) to win fame ______________________

b) to win hands down ______________________

c) to win s.o.'s heart/love ______________________

d) to win the day/field ______________________

e) to win one's bread ______________________

f) to win s.o. over to s.th. ______________________

g) Ok, you win ______________________

write

331 **Fill in the right form of the verb: / Setzen Sie die korrekte Verbform ein:**

a) I'm trying to ________ a book. It's something I have never done before.

b) When the couple lived far apart from each other they ________ letters every day.

c) Mother has ________ a long list of things she needs to buy.

332 **Form meaningful sentences: / Bilden Sie sinnvolle Sätze:**

a) In March I will	written	four tests in a row.
b) All the instructions are	wrote	on this slip of paper.
c) Not knowing the answer I	write	a lot of nonsense.

333 **Idioms - do you know their meaning? / Redewendungen - kennen Sie ihre Bedeutung?**

a) That's nothing to write home about ______________________

b) written in water ______________________

c) to write s.th. off ______________________

d) to write shorthand ______________________

e) to write s.o. down as ______________________

f) to write in for s.th. ______________________

g) to write s.th. up ______________________

Weitere unregelmäßige Verben

abide	abode/abided	abode/abided	bleiben, wohnen
arise	arose	arisen	sich erheben
bear	bore	borne (born)	tragen (*born* – geboren)
befall	befell	befallen	widerfahren
beget	begot	begotten	(er)zeugen
behold	beheld	beheld	erblicken
bereave	bereaved/ bereft	bereaved/ bereft	berauben
beseech	besought	besought	ersuchen
beset	beset	beset	besetzen, einschließen
betake	betook	betaken	(sich) begeben
bethink	bethought	bethought	(sich) besinnen auf
bid	bade/bid	bidden/bid	gebieten, lassen
broadcast	broadcast	broadcast	per Rundfunk senden
browbeat	browbeat	browbeaten	tyrannisieren
cast	cast	cast	werfen
chide	chid	chidden/chid	schelten
cleave	clove/cleft	cloven/cleft	spalten
cling	clung	clung	festhalten
dwell	dwelt	dwelt	wohnen
flee	fled	fled	fliehen
forebear	forebore	foreborne	sich enthalten
foresee	foresaw	foreseen	voraussehen, absehen
foretell	foretold	foretold	voraussagen

forsake	forsook	forsaken	aufgeben
freeze	froze	frozen	gefrieren
gild	gilded/gilt	gilded/gilt	vergolden
gird	girded/girt	girded/girt	(um)gürten
grind	ground	ground	mahlen
hang	hung	hung	(auf)hängen,
	hanged	hanged	(er)hängen, henken
heave	heaved/hove	heaved/hove	heben, hieven
hew	hewed	hewed/hewn	hauen, hacken
kneel	knelt	knelt	knien
knit	knitted/knit	knitted/knit	stricken
lade	laded	laden	laden
lean	leant	leant	lehnen
melt	melted	melted/molten	schmelzen
mistake	mistook	mistaken	verwechseln
mow	mowed	mown	mähen
overbear	overbore	overborne	überwältigen, überstehen
overcome	overcame	overcome	überwältigen
partake	partook	partaken	teilnehmen
rend	rent	rent	zerreißen
rid	rid	rid	befreien
ring	rang	rung	läuten
rive	rived	rived/riven	(sich) spalten
saw	sawed	sawn	sägen
sew	sewed	sewn	nähen
shear	sheared	sheared/shorn	scheren
shoe	shod	shod	beschuhen, beschlagen
slay	slew	slain	erschlagen
sling	slung	slung	schleudern
slink	slunk	slunk	schleichen
slit	slit	slit	schlitzen

smite	smote	smitten	treffen, schlagen
sow	sowed	sown	säen
speed	sped	sped	eilen, sich sputen
spell	spelt	spelt	buchstabieren
spill	spilt	spilt	verschütten
spit	spat	spat	speien, spucken
spoil	spoilt	spoilt	verderben
sting	stung	stung	stechen
stink	stank/stunk	stunk	stinken
strew	strewed	strewn, strewed	streuen
stride	strode	stridden	schreiten
string	strung	strung	aufreihen
strive	strove	striven	streben
swear	swore	sworn	schwören
swell	swelled	swollen	schwellen
swing	swung	swung	schwingen
tear	tore	torn	zerreißen
thrive	throve, thrived	thriven, thrived	gedeihen
thrust	thrust	thrust	stoßen
tread	trod	trodden, trod	treten
upset	upset	upset	umwerfen; beunruhigen
wake	woke, waked	woken, waked	wachen, wach bleiben
wear	wore	worn	(Kleidung) tragen
weave	wove	woven	weben
weep	wept	wept	weinen
wind	wound	wound	winden
withdraw	withdrew	withdrawn	(sich) zurückziehen
withhold	withheld	withheld	zurückhalten
withstand	withstood	withstood	widerstehen
wring	wrung	wrung	(Hände) ringen; (Wäsche) auswringen

Lösungen

awake – aufwachen/wecken

1 a) awake b) awoke/awaked

2 The correct sentences are:
b) He awoke his wife with his coughing. c) The chicken have awaked long before me today. e) The chicken have awoken long before me today.

3 Redewendungen:
a) sich einer Sache bewußt werden; Der Gangster wurde sich bewußt, daß er der Polizei niemals entkommen würde. b) jemandem etwas zum Bewußtsein bringen; Die Lehrerin machte mich auf meine Fehler aufmerksam.

Merke:
Es gibt auch das regelmäßig gebildete Verb *to awaken*:
z.B. The customer's behaviour awakened her anger.
Wie zu *awake* werden die Formen von *wake* gebildet:
wake, woke, woken - aufwachen, wecken

!

be – sein

4 The correct sentences are:
a) The school this girl went to was a very traditional one. b) My grandmother is wonderful, she sends me a letter each week. c) This theatre performance has been the best I have seen so far.

5 a) is b) was c) been

6 Redewendungen:
a) im Begriff sein, etwas zu tun b) ganz Ohr sein c) bei vollem Verstand sein d) im Bilde bzw. informiert sein e) um ganz sicher zu gehen

beat – schlagen

7 a) beat b) beat c) beaten

8 The correct sentences are:
b) The man has beaten his dog because he had run away. c) In a sportsgame the winner beats the loser.

9 Redewendungen:
a) Das darf doch nicht war sein! b) Das ist doch die Höhe! c) um die Sache herumreden d) die Frist einhalten

become – werden

10 a) become b) became c) become

11 The correct sentences are:
a) The floor becomes dirty when you walk on it with muddy boots. b) His work became more and more difficult. c) After her long studies she has become a doctor, finally.

12 Redewendung:
Es ist zur Regel geworden, daß alle ihre dreckigen Teller selber abräumen.

Merke:
become bedeutet nicht dt. *bekommen*, sondern *werden*.

begin – beginnen

13 a) begin b) began c) begun

14 The correct sentences are:
a) We will begin painting as soon as the walls have dried off. b) When their parents left the children began to prepare for the party. c) Not only had they begun to roll up the carpets, they had also begun to drag away the rest of the furniture.

15 Redewendungen:
a) Nun, zunächst einmal möchte ich Ihnen den Direktor unserer kleinen Firma vorstellen. b) Mein Vater betet jeden Morgen, denn er glaubt, daß "gut begonnen halb gewonnen" ist. c) Mit diesem Satz auf den Lippen gab es nichts, was sie nicht in Angriff genommen hätte.

bend – biegen; beugen

16 a) bend b) bent c) bent

17 The correct sentences are:
a) The teacher bent down to pick up the chalk. c) Her head had been bent in sorrow from the day he left.

18 Redewendungen:
a) sich unterwerfen b) sich einer Aufgabe widmen c) verbiegen d) sich übermäßig anstrengen, sich sehr bemühen etwas zu tun

bet – wetten

19 a) bet b) bet/betted c) bet/betted

20 The correct sentences are:
a) I bet you twenty pounds that I will beat you at golf next time. b) Everybody betted/bet on the same horse.

21 Redewendungen:
a) Na, und ob!/Aber sicher! b) Darauf kannst du Gift nehmen!

bind – binden

22 a) binds b) bound c) bound

23 The correct sentence is:
a) All the members of our club must be bound to secrecy.

24 Redewendungen:
a) zwangsläufig etwas tun müssen; Er mußte ja etwas Dummes tun. b) Das mußte ja passieren. c) Ich mußte sagen, daß ich das nicht lustig finde. d) ganz aufgehen in etwas, ganz in Anspruch genommen sein von etwas; Man kann jedoch sehen, daß er von irgend etwas ganz in Anspruch genommen sein muß.

> **Merke:**
> to be snowbound - eingeschneit, von der Außenwelt abgeschnitten sein

bite – beißen

25 a) bites b) bit c) bitten

26 The correct sentences are:
a) He spent hours fishing but nothing would ever bite. b) Heavy smoke was biting my eyes. c) His face looked terrible - it was badly bitten by the mosquitoes.

27 a) sich eine Bemerkung verkneifen b) ins Gras beißen c) seinen Ärger hinunterschlucken d) wer anderen eine Grube gräbt, fällt selbst hinein. e) ein gebranntes Kind scheut das Feuer.

bleed – bluten

28 a) bleed b) bled c) bled

29 The correct sentences are:
a) The wound bled so badly that she fainted. b) Ronald has cut his finger; now it is bleeding badly.

30 a) ich habe großes Mitleid mit dir; mir kommen gleich die Tränen (iron.) b) für etwas schwer bluten müssen c) jemanden völlig ausnehmen; sein ganzes Geld abknöpfen; jemanden auspressen

blow – blasen

31 a) blows b) blew c) blown

32 a) She had a cold and blew her nose all the time. b) The storm has finally blown over; it has taken down our roof. c) Could you please blow the candle out?

33 a) das Fähnchen nach dem Wind drehen, unbeständig sein b) Dampf ablassen, sich austoben c) vor Wut explodieren, in die Luft gehen d) die Beherrschung verlieren e) etwas aufbauschen

> **Merke:**
> to blow the whistle on s.o. (bes. AE) - jemanden ‚verpfeifen'

break – brechen

34 a) break b) broke c) broken

35 b) She bumped against the shelf so that five wineglasses broke. c) We were very disappointed with our friends because they had broken their word.

36 a) das Eis brechen; Ihre lustige Bemerkung brach das Eis. b) etwas machen, was noch niemand gemacht hat; Neuland betreten c) jemandem eine Neuigkeit schonend mitteilen; Wir mußten seinen Eltern die Nachricht über seinen Unfall schonend mitteilen. d) eine Beziehung beenden

bring – bringen

37 a) bring b) brought c) brought

38 The correct sentences are:
a) As she hasn't brought back the car I can't drive home yet. b) Come and bring your friends along with you. c) Their conversation brought him down to earth.

39 a) jemanden zur Vernunft bringen b) jemanden auf den Boden der Tatsachen zurückholen c) eine Veränderung bewirken/mit sich bringen d) etwas zur Sprache bringen e) Zuschauer zu begeistertem Applaus hinreißen f) etwas aufdecken, ans Tageslicht bringen g) jemanden zur Strecke bringen h) etwas ins Spiel bringen i) etwas ans Tageslicht bringen

build – bauen

40 a) build b) built c) built

41 The correct sentences are:
a) The Eskimo boy has built the igloo out of icy blocks of snow. b) Do not build on him, he never does what he says. c) Rome wasn't built in a day.

42 a) seine Hoffnungen setzen auf b) Luftschlösser bauen c) auf Sand gebaut

burn – brennen, verbrennen

43 a) burn b) burnt/burned c) burnt/burned

44 The correct sentences are:
a) In poor countries people burn their rubbish in their backyards. b) In India the dead have always been burnt/burned. c) At Easter we lit a big bonfire and burnt/burned lots of dry brambles.

45 a) alle Brücken hinter sich abbrechen b) bis spät in die Nacht aufbleiben und arbeiten (lernen) c) sich übernehmen; sich Tag und Nacht keine Ruhe gönnen d) völlig abbrennen (Haus)

Merke:
to burn s.o. up (AE) - jemanden ausschimpfen
to get burned up (AE) - wütend werden

burst – bersten, platzen

46 a) burst b) burst c) burst

47 The correct sentences are:
a) Suddenly my mother burst into the room. b) With the exam in my hand I was bursting with pride. c) He is so fat that he bursts out of his jeans.

48 a) in Flammen aufgehen b) in Gelächter/Tränen ausbrechen c) ins Laub schießen (Bäume) d) sich vor Lachen schütteln e) voller Stolz sein f) vor Energie strotzen

buy – kaufen

49 a) buy b) bought c) bought

50 The correct sentences are:
a) He bought the house from his best friend. d) I have forgotten to buy some milk.

51 a) Zeit gewinnen; Indem er eine Menge Unsinn redete, versuchte er Zeit zu gewinnen. b) etwas ganz billig erstehen c) Das glaube ich dir nicht!

catch – fangen

52 a) catch b) caught c) caught

53 The correct sentences are:
a) At last I caught up with her. b) My uncle always catches many fish during his holidays. c) Are you able to catch a very fast ball well?

54 a) jemanden auf frischer Tat ertappen b) jemandes Aufmerksamkeit auf sich lenken c) wieder zu Atem kommen d) jemanden kurz erblicken e) jemanden einholen

choose – (aus)wählen

55 a) choose b) chose c) chosen

56 The correct forms are:
a) chosen b) chose c) chooses

57 a) Tu, was dir beliebt/gefällt! b) Es ist kaum ein Unterschied zwischen ihnen. c) Es bleibt uns keine andere Wahl, als es zu tun.

> **Merke:**
> the chosen people - das auserwählte Volk (Bibel)

come – kommen

58 a) Come b) came c) come

59 a) Daddy, will Father Christmas come to us again this year?

60 a) geschehen, passieren, zustandekommen b) kurz vorbeischauen, jemanden besuchen c) nützlich sein, wie gerufen kommen d) in Mode kommen e) abgehen, sich lösen (z.B. Knopf) f) sich ernsthaft auseinandersetzen mit etwas g) zu dem Schluß kommen, daß h) zur Besinnung kommen, wieder zur Vernunft kommen i) zur Sache kommen j) sich einigen mit jemandem k) etwas bewältigen, mit etwas fertig werden l) unter Beschuß geraten, mit Worten angegriffen werden m) daherkommen mit, präsentieren (z.B. Idee, Plan, Lösung) n) wenn ich es mir recht überlege... o) was auch immer geschieht; komme, was wolle p) in den kommenden Jahren q) Hör schon auf damit! Gib nicht so an! Tu nicht so!

cost – kosten

61 a) costs b) cost c) cost

62 The correct sentences are:
a) This is a nice shirt. How much does it cost? b) Writing this book costs me much time. c) His fancy for fast cars has cost him his life.

63 a) jemanden teuer zu stehen kommen b) ein Heidengeld kosten c) einen zu hohen Preis haben

Merke:
In der Bedeutung von *Kosten kalkulieren, veranschlagen* wird die ansonsten unübliche Form *costed at* verwendet: z.B. *The working hours were costed at 200 pounds*.

creep – kriechen; schleichen

64 a) creep b) crept c) crept

65 The correct sentences are:
a) He crept on all fours over the creaking boards. b) It made my flesh creep to watch this movie. c) Due to exhaustion I crept the last few steps.

66 a) jemandem eine Gänsehaut machen, Angst machen b) sich bei jemandem einschmeicheln c) jemanden beschleichen (z.B. Angst) d) langsam steigen (z.B. Auflage einer Zeitung, Preise etc.) e) sich an jemanden heranschleichen f) wieder angekrochen kommen g) die Zeit geht dahin

Merke:
creeper - Kletterpflanze; a creep - Kriecher, Schleimer

cut – schneiden

67 a) cut b) cut c) cut

68 The correct forms are:
a) Mary needs to have her hair cut. b) You have to cut this piece of cardboard in two. It's too big.

69 a) etwas verringern, herabsetzen, einschränken (z.B. Produktion, Ausgaben) b) die Kurven schneiden (mit einem Auto) c) sich nach den Verhältnissen richten d) um es kurz zu machen e) ein zweischneidiges Schwert sein, seine Vor- und Nachteile haben f) Hör auf damit! g) jemanden ‚schneiden', links liegen lassen, nicht beachten, völlig ignorieren h) jemanden sehr betrüben, ins Herz treffen i) jemanden zurechtweisen, den Kopf zurechtsetzen j) jemanden enterben k) für etwas wie geschaffen sein l) jemandem den Boden unter den Füßen wegziehen m) jemanden unterbieten (Geschäft)

Merke:
to cut up (AE) - angeben, Quatsch machen

deal – (be)handeln, verteilen

70 a) deals b) dealt

71 b) My sister's shop deals in cowboy boots.

72 a) Karten austeilen; Könntest du die Karten ein kleines bißchen schneller austeilen, bitte. b) mit jemandem vekehren, zu tun haben; Sie fühlte sich in seiner Gegenwart so unwohl, daß sie nie mehr was mit ihm zu tun haben wollte. c) sich mit etwas befassen; mit etwas fertig werden; zu Rande kommen; erledigen; Er wird damit sehr gut fertig.

dig – graben

73 a) digging b) dug c) dug

74 b) In the Sahara you have to dig very deep to find water. c) He has been digging up the whole garden for me.

75 a) Er schaufelte sich sein eigenes Grab. b) etwas aufstöbern c) Hau rein! (Aufforderung zum Essen)

dive – (ein)tauchen

76 a) dive b) dived/dove c) dived

Merke:
Nur im AE ist die Form *dove* üblich, in England ist das Verb regelmäßig.

77 The correct sentences are:
a) The girl had lost an earring in the swimming pool and five boys dived/dove into the water to find it for her. b) How deep can you dive?

78 a) Hau rein! (Aufforderung zum Essen; vgl. ‚dig in!') b) in der Menge untertauchen; Der hübsche Mann tauchte in der Menge unter und verschwand aus meinem Blick. c) nach dem Ball hechten; Der Torwart hechtete nach dem Ball, doch er konnte ihn nicht mehr fangen.

do – tun, machen

79 a) do b) did c) done

80 a) Can you do anything about it? b) It's not what she did, it's how she did it that annoys me. c) What have I done that he treats me like this?

81 a) etwas beseitigen; abschaffen b) mit jemandem Geschäfte machen c) den eigenen Beitrag leisten, die Pflicht tun d) ich könnte etwas gut gebrauchen, etwas würde mir gut tun e) jemandem einen Gefallen tun f) jemandem schaden, etwas antun g) jemanden umbringen h) erledigt sein, am Ende sein i) auf etwas verzichten j) jemandem/einer Sache gerecht werden k) geschirrspülen l) sich herrichten, zurechtmachen m) sich schminken n) Da ist nichts zu machen, kommt nicht in Frage! o) Das genügt, das reicht!

> **Merke:**
> Das Verb *do* wird sehr häufig auch als Hilfsverb gebraucht!

draw – zeichnen; ziehen

82 a) draw b) drew c) drawn

83 a) Sometimes donkeys still draw the plough. b) Before he drew the tiger he watched him for hours. c) I thank you for having drawn my portrait so nicely.

84 a) nahe heranfahren an etwas b) sich auseinanderleben (Personen) c) jemandes Aufmerksamkeit auf etwas lenken d) etwas zu Ende bringen, abschließen e) in Anspruch nehmen, zurückgreifen auf (z.B. Ersparnisse) f) einen Scheck einlösen g) die Grenze ziehen, bei etwas nicht mehr mitmachen h) näher kommen (zeitlich und örtlich)

dream – träumen

85 a) dream b) dreamed/dreamt c) dreamed/dreamt

86 The correct sentences are:
a) She never dreamed of seeing him again. He had been gone so long. c) She never dreamt of seeing him again. He had been gone so long. e) In some nights I dream of the loveliest places. f) He must have dreamed with his eyes open. h) He must have dreamt with his eyes open.

87 a) Zeit verträumen, vertun b) sich etwas zusammenphantasieren, sich etwas ausdenken

drink – trinken

88 a) drinks b) drank c) drunk

89 a) With a fever you should drink a lot of herb tea. b) All the guests drank to the couple's health. c) No more coffee for me. I have drunk five cups already.

90 a) etwas versaufen (Geld); etwas im Alkohol ertränken (Sorgen) b) jemanden unter den Tisch trinken c) jemandes Worte förmlich aufsaugen d) Luft einatmen, einsaugen e) den Ausblick genießen

drive – fahren; treiben

91 a) Drive b) drove c) driven

92 The correct sentences are:
a) Most people here learn to drive at 18. b) When my sister moved I drove the van. c) He had finally driven the nail into the wall.

93 a) jemanden wahnsinnig, verrückt machen b) jemanden verrückt machen, auf die Palme bringen c) jemanden verrückt machen d) jemandem etwas klar machen e) auf etwas hinauswollen, auf etwas anspielen; f) jemanden in die Enge treiben

eat – essen

94 a) eat b) ate c) eaten

95 a) I can't possibly eat another piece of cake, thank you. b) They ate at a very fine restaurant on her birthday. c) My father has eaten his favourite meal – potato soup.

96 a) wie ein Spatz essen, sehr wenig essen b) wie ein Scheunendrescher essen c) einen Besen fressen d) Gesagtes zurücknehmen, widerrufen e) essen gehen f) Was für eine Laus ist ihm über die Leber gelaufen? Was hat er denn?

fall – fallen

97 a) fall b) fell c) fallen

98 a) Try not to fall on your knees when you go skating. b) He fell for her at the very first sight. c) The temperature of all the sick children has fallen.

99 a) sich in jemanden verlieben b) sich in jemanden verlieben c) nichts werden, ins Wasser fallen d) schiefgehen, ausfallen e) auf etwas zurückgreifen, einen Rückhalt haben an etwas f) hinter jemandem zurückbleiben, ins Hintertreffen geraten g) sich überschlagen, etwas zu tun; etwas mit besonderem Eifer tun

feed – füttern

100 a) feeds b) fed c) fed

101 a) She is so fed up with her living situation that she will move soon. d) Animals need to be fed every day. e) Will you feed the cats or shall I do it?

102 a) Kind stillen b) etwas essen, sich ernähren von c) seine Augen weiden an etwas d) genug von etwas/jemandem haben; Ich hoffe sie geht bald, ich habe wirklich genug von ihr. e) sich den eigenen Ast absägen

feel – (sich an)fühlen

103 a) feel b) felt c) felt

104 a) She could feel the snake gliding over her foot. b) My brother felt around for his glasses. Without them he couldn't see a thing. c) I have felt the earth move under my feet.

105 a) Lust haben, etwas zu tun b) sich zu etwas aufraffen können, in der Stimmung sein zu etwas; einer Sache gewachsen sein c) sich fehl am Platze fühlen d) sich vorwärts tasten, vorsichtig vorgehen e) jemand tut einem/einer leid

fight – (be)kämpfen

106 a) fight b) fought c) fought

107 a) Why do we always fight over unimportant things? b) I think that fighting is boring. c) The children fought over the doll.

108 a) etwas untereinander ausfechten b) Tränen unterdrücken c) eine verlorene Schlacht schlagen d) mit aller Kraft um etwas kämpfen e) sich seinen Weg bahnen, sich durchschlagen

find – finden

109 a) find b) found c) found

110 b) Where have you found her? c) Find yourself a husband and settle down, he told me.

111 a) jemanden ertappen; Ich ertappte sie. b) sich eingewöhnen, zurecht kommen; Er gewöhnte sich ein. c) Du mußt es nehmen, wie es ist.

Merke:
Man darf dieses Verb nicht verwechseln mit: found/founded/founded - gründen.

flung – werfen, schleudern

112 a) flings b) flung c) flung

113 The correct sentences are:
a) Utterly exhausted Joan flung herself into the chair.
b) Oh, I'm so terribly late. I'm sure she'll fling the flowers back into my face when I finally reach our meeting point.

114 a) sich auf jemanden stürzen; sich jemandem an den Hals werfen b) jemandem etwas ins Gesicht schleudern (Bemerkung)

fly – fliegen

115 a) fly b) flew, flying c) flown

116 a) Tomorrow my best friend will fly to England. b) The birds flew away when she clapped her hands. c) This morning his balloon has flown away with the wind.

117 a) ehrgeizig sein, hochgesteckte Ziele haben, hoch hinauswollen b) auf jemanden losgehen c) aus der Haut fahren d) grob werden gegen jemanden e) ich muß schleunigst weg

Merke:
Man darf dieses Verb nicht verwechseln mit: flow/flowed/flowed-fließen.

forbid – verbieten

118 a) forbid b) forbade c) forbidden

119 a) He forbade you to buy this coat? Why? b) I forbid that you ever meet her again. c) She has forbidden her children to play near the road.

120 Redewendungen:
a) Gott möge uns davor behüten, daß b) Der Himmel möge uns davor bewahren c) Gott bewahre!

Merke:
forbidding - abstoßend, widerwärtig; bedrohlich

forget – vergessen

121 a) forgets b) forgot c) forgotten

122 a) You can't have forgotten the tickets, can you? b) He promised never to forget her no matter how long they would be parted. c) Let's forget what happened and start anew, shall we?

123 a) sich vergessen, aus der Rolle fallen b) Vergiß es! Es ist nicht wichtig! c) Reg dich nicht auf!

forgive – vergeben, verzeihen

124 a) She swore never to forgive him for this insulting speech. b) He usually forgave easily even if one hurt him. c) We had forgiven and forgotten the matter long ago.

125 a) forgive b) forgave c) forgiven

126 Redewendung:
jemandem eine Schuld erlassen; Er erläßt ihr eine Schuld.

get – bekommen, werden

127 a) gets b) got c) got/gotten (AE)

128 The correct sentences are:
a) My little sister always gets what she wants. d) Look, he has got/gotten her a lovely present. e) Please, be careful with your sneezing and coughing. I don't want to get the flu as well.

129 a) etwas ‚rüberbringen', etwas verständlich machen b) mit jemanden auskommen

c) vorankommen, Karriere machen d) keine Grenzen mehr kennen e) zur Sache kommen f) in Schwierigkeiten geraten g) sich etwas angewöhnen h) mit jemandem Kontakt aufnehmen, jemanden anrufen i) außer Kontrolle geraten j) etwas/jemanden loswerden k) etwas überwinden l) die Oberhand über jemanden gewinnen, jemanden ausstechen m) den Dreh 'rauskriegen n) jemanden in die Klauen bekommen o) jemandem auf die Nerven gehen p) in Gang kommen, in Gang bringen q) ungestraft davonkommen mit etwas r) entlassen werden s) etwas falsch verstehen t) etwas hinter sich bringen u) Wie geht's? – Es geht so, ich komme so zurecht. v) Was ist denn in dich gefahren?

Merke:
Im AE heißt das Past participle meist *gotten.*

give – geben

130 a) Give b) gave c) given

131 The correct sentences are:
a) After the third beer he gave me the car keys. b) She has given her a terrible fright. c) Never give up before you haven't tried everything.

132 a) jemandem nachgeben b) jemandem bei etwas helfen c) zeugen von etwas d) gebären, zur Welt bringen e) einem Gefühl Luft machen f) etwas verraten, ausplaudern g) eine Gänsehaut bekommen, erschauern, jemanden kalt überlaufen h) Das glaubst du doch selbst nicht! i) verursachen j) Das ist mir völlig egal! k) jemandem herzliche Grüße bestellen l) jemandem ordentlich die Meinung sagen m) einen Vortrag halten n) alles geben für etwas o) für tot gehalten werden p) jemanden verprügeln, jemandem die Meinung sagen

go – gehen (fahren, reisen)

133 a) Go b) went c) gone

134 The correct sentences are:
a) Don't go away! I can't bear to be alone. c) Every day of the summer I went into my garden to watch the plants grow. f) He has not gone yet. I can still hear his voice downstairs.

135 a) etwas angehen b) schiefgehen (Sache); sich irren (Person) c) die Kosten teilen d) spazierengehen e) zum einen Ohr hinein, zum anderen hinaus f) sich besondere Mühe geben g) vor die Hunde gehen h) mit jemandem übereinstimmen i) sich für etwas interessieren, sich mit etwas befassen j) nicht aufhören, über etwas zu reden k) etwas Ungewöhnliches tun l) aus der Mode kommen m) mit der Zeit gehen n) zu weit gehen o) Na also! p) Das gilt für euch alle. q) Das versteht sich von selbst. r) Alles ist erlaubt/möglich.

grow – wachsen

136 a) grows b) grew c) grown

137 a) The puppies grew up so quickly. b) Grandmother planted these firs 29 years ago. Look, how they have grown. c) In this soil everything will grow.

138 a) alt/dunkel/. . . werden b) sich auseinander entwickeln, sich auseinander leben c) sich jemandem entfremden d) zahlreicher werden e) weiser werden f) sich entwickeln zu, heranwachsen zu g) in etwas hineinwachsen (Arbeit) h) aus etwas herauswachsen; zu alt für etwas werden i) eine Gewohnheit ablegen j) zusammenwachsen, sich besser verstehen k) sich immer mehr an etwas gewöhnen; jemandem ans Herz wachsen l) Geld fällt nicht vom Himmel.

have – haben

139 a) have b) had c) had

140 a) My friend has a lorry we can borrow when we move house. d) Do you have enough money on you to pay the bill?

141 a) Ich sollte es besser tun; Es wäre besser, wenn ich es täte b) etwas ausprobieren, versuchen c) einen Versuch machen mit etwas d) etwas beherrschen, gut können e) in jemanden verknallt sein f) jemandem grollen g) jemanden gern mögen, eine Vorliebe haben für jemanden h) bei etwas mitzureden haben i) mit jemandem sprechen j) sich mit jemandem streiten k) das gewisse Etwas haben, das Zeug haben zu l) zu Tode erschrocken sein m) bei etwas mitmischen n) etwas parat haben; etwas gut beherrschen o) seinen Willen/Kopf durchsetzen p) einen Riesenspaß haben q) etwas bereinigen mit jemandem, etwas in Ordnung bringen, klarstellen r) eine Überraschung parat haben s) viele Eisen im Feuer haben t) jemanden bemitleiden

Merke:
Das Verb *have* wird natürlich auch als Hilfsverb gebraucht!

hear – hören

142 a) hear b) heard c) heard

143 a) Have you ever heard such beautiful music? b) He seems not to hear me. Is he deaf? c) Grandfather had heard a child crying and found this little boy sitting all by himself.

144 a) jemanden ausreden lassen b) Nachricht erhalten von jemandem c) etwas erfahren d) wir wollten nichts davon wissen.

hide – (sich) verstecken

145 a) hide b) hid c) hidden

146 a) Come, let's play hide and seek! b) Mum has hidden the easter eggs very well. c) My brother hid in this corner and got stuck.

147 a) die Gefühle verbergen; Janet gelang es nie, ihre Gefühle zu verbergen. b) sich verstecken

Merke:
Das *Versteckspiel* heißt auf englisch *hide-and-seek.*

hit – schlagen; treffen

148 a) hits b) hit c) hit

149 a) The pot hit the floor with a loud bang. d) He hit ten of the nails right on the head and missed only the eleventh. Now he has a blue thumb.

150 a) den Nagel auf den Kopf treffen b) mit jemandem schnell warm werden, sich gut verstehen mit jemandem c) Du hast es richtig getroffen/erraten; So ist es! Genau! d) vor Wut in die Luft gehen e) abreisen, aufbrechen, sich auf den Weg machen f) zurückschlagen, sich verteidigen, einen Gegenschlag unternehmen, jemandem Kontra geben g) jemandem einen Schlag versetzen h) sich in die Falle hauen, schlafen gehen

hold – halten

151 a) hold b) held c) held

152 a) All I heard was the operator's voice saying 'Hold the line...' b) He held on to the branch for dear life. c) She had held the baby as if it were made of glass.

153 a) jemanden in Schach halten; etwas unter Kontrolle halten b) den Mund halten c) eine Versammlung abhalten d) Wahlen abhalten e) sich behaupten f) festhalten an etwas g) den Atem anhalten h) jemanden hochschätzen/geringschätzen, hochachten/geringachten i) eine niedrige Meinung von etwas haben j) jemanden verantwortlich machen k) jemandem etwas übelnehmen l) etwas billigen, einverstanden sein mit etwas m) neben jemandem bestehen können, sich behaupten gegen jemanden n) etwas verschweigen, vorenthalten o) zutreffen auf, gelten für p) der Ansicht sein, daß . . . q) jemanden liebhaben r) nicht stichhaltig sein s) Bitte bleiben Sie am Apparat! t) Warte mal! Moment mal! u) Halt! Stop!

hurt – (sich) verletzen, wehtun

154 a) hurts b) hurt c) hurt

155 a) This bird can't fly. It must have hurt its wing. d) By saying these things you hurt me deeply. e) He is such a sweet boy. He couldn't hurt a fly.

156 a) Er würde keiner Fliege etwas zuleide tun. b) jemandes Gefühle verletzen, jemanden kränken c) das schadet nichts.

keep – (be)halten; aufbewahren

157 a) keep b) kept c) kept

158 a) Keep your thoughts to yourself. I don't want to hear them. b) You keep your pearls locked in a safe, don't you? c) Have you kept the group together all the time? d) My father kept me away from bad influence as long as he could.

159 a) dranbleiben an einer Arbeit, weitermachen mit etwas b) mit jemandem mithalten c) die Daumen drücken d) Halt die Ohren steif! e) ein Auge auf etwas haben, etwas im Auge behalten f) jemanden auf Distanz halten g) jemanden in Schach halten (vgl.

to hold s.o. at bay) h) etwas nicht vergessen, an etwas denken i) in Kontakt bleiben mit jemandem j) etwas weiterhin tun; fortfahren, etwas zu tun k) ruhig bleiben, sich ruhig verhalten l) jemandem Gesellschaft leisten m) etwas verfolgen, sich auf dem laufenden halten n) Buch führen über etwas o) sich nicht blicken lassen p) Weiter so! q) jemanden davon abhalten, etwas zu tun r) den Schein wahren s) jemanden warten lassen t) jemanden über etwas im Ungewissen lassen u) gelassen bleiben v) sich fernhalten von etwas w) fit, in Form bleiben x) jemanden in die Schranken weisen y) ich werde dich nicht lange aufhalten

know – kennen; wissen

160 a) know b) knew c) known

161 a) I have never known a happier person than her. b) She couldn't know what would be asked in the exam. c) He was sure he knew her from somewhere else.

162 a) etwas auswendig können b) etwas in- und auswendig kennen c) Bescheid wissen, sich auskennen d) zwei Dinge auseinander halten können e) auf seinen Vorteil aus sein, sich beliebt machen f) nicht, daß ich wüßte g) soviel ich weiß

lay – legen

163 a) lay b) laid c) laid

164 The correct sentences are:
b) I laid the blame on him but I was wrong. d) Would he have laid hands on you? I don't think so. e) The police laid a trap to catch the thief.

165 a) den Tisch decken b) die Karten auf den Tisch legen c) etwas betonen, hervorheben d) Anspruch erheben auf etwas e) etwas zu dick auftragen, übertreiben f) jemandem die Schuld für etwas zuschieben g) etwas in die Finger bekommen, erwischen h) Pläne machen

lead – führen, leiten

166 a) lead b) led c) led

167 The correct sentences are:
a) This teacher leads her class quite well. b) I'm sure she led a double life in her youth. c) Please, lead me out of this labyrinth of streets.

168 a) den Weg zeigen, vorrangehen b) auf den falschen Weg führen, fehlleiten, vom richtigen Weg wegführen c) jemanden auf den Arm nehmen d) jemanden an der Nase herumführen e) jemanden völlig beherrschen, an der Kandare haben, unter seiner Fuchtel haben f) auf einen Ort zuführen

leap – springen

169 a) leap b) leapt/leaped c) leapt/leaped

170 The correct sentences are:
a) He went two steps back and then he leaped over the hedge as if it was nothing.
d) He was scared that the big dog would leap the fence as well.

171 a) die Gelegenheit sofort wahrnehmen b) sich auf ein Angebot stürzen c) jemandem ins Auge springen, hervorstechen d) jemandem schlagartig in den Sinn kommen e) Erst denken, dann handeln! f) die Herzen höher schlagen lassen

Merke:
Leap-year heißt auf deutsch *Schaltjahr*

learn – lernen; erfahren

172 a) learn b) learnt/learned c) learnt/learned

173 The correct sentences are:
a) How did you learn to speak English so well? b) My dog has learned/learnt to run before a sledge. c) Most children learned/learnt from experience whatever they know of the world.

174 a) etwas auswendig lernen b) etwas aus bitterer Erfahrung lernen c) einen Denkzettel bekommen, seine Lektion erteilt bekommen d) man lernt nie aus.

leave – (ver)lassen

175 a) Leave b) left c) left

176 The correct sentences are:
a) If he leaves me I'll never be the same. b) Her friends had left the pub before she arrived. c) I left my backpack in the train.

177 Redewendungen
a) alle Hebel in Bewegung setzen, nichts unversucht lassen b) jemanden in Ruhe lassen c) viel zu wünschen übrig lassen d) jemanden im Stich lassen e) jemanden kalt lassen, nicht interessieren, gelassen hinnehmen f) es dabei belassen, bewenden lassen g) etwas dem Zufall überlassen h) ignoriert werden, übergangen werden i) übrig sein j) nach Edingburgh aufbrechen k) postlagernd

lend – (ver)leihen

178 a) lend b) lent c) lent

179 The correct sentences are:
a) Lend me your ear and I'll sing you a song. c) Our grass had to be cut so a friend lent a lawnmower to us. f) It's raining cats and dogs. Could you lend me your umbrella?

180 a) jemandem zur Hand gehen bei etwas; b) Hilfe leisten; Früher ging er seinem Vater immer bei der Gartenarbeit zur Hand. c) sich hergeben zu etwas d) sich eignen für etwas; e) jemandem Gehör schenken

let – lassen

181 a) let b) let c) let

182 a) Let him go. He didn't do any harm. b) She never lets anyone look into the pots when she is cooking. c) After having asked him numerous questions they finally let him go.

183 a) ein Zimmer vermieten b) die Katze aus dem Sack lassen c) geschweige denn d) eine Bemerkung fallen lassen e) Dampf ablassen, vor Wut explodieren f) sich gehen lassen; aus sich herausgehen g) sich etwas einbrocken; sich einlassen auf h) aus sich herausgehen, sich ungezwungen benehmen, sich austoben i) etwas loslassen j) jemanden im Stich lassen; enttäuschen k) jemanden in ein Geheimnis einweihen l) jemanden laufen lassen, davonkommen lassen m) jemandem rutscht ein Geheimnis heraus, sich verplappern n) verraten, daß . . . o) mal sehen, ich muß mal überlegen . . .

lie – liegen

184 a) lies b) lay c) laid, (lain)

185 The correct sentences are:
a) She was so tired that all she wanted was to lie down and sleep. c) The house lay in a very quiet street.

186 a) es liegt bei dir; es ist deine Sache. b) schwer auf jemandem lasten c) morgens lange im Bett bleiben d) sich in einem Sessel zurücklehnen e) in Trümmern liegen f) sich versteckt halten g) eine Verpflichtung haben h) jemandem bevorstehen i) Schlafende Hunde soll man nicht wecken. j) schauen, wie die Dinge liegen; schauen, wie es steht k) wissen, wo der eigene Vorteil liegt

Merke:
Dieses Verb darf man nicht verwechseln mit:
lie/lied/lied - lügen;
lay/laid/laid - legen

light – anzünden; beleuchten

187 a) lights b) lit/lighted c) lit/lighted

188 a) With my torch I lit up the whole room. b) With my torch I lighted up the whole room. e) Shall I light your cigarette for you?

189 a) landen auf etwas; etwas durch Zufall entdecken b) angeheitert sein, beschwipst sein; Nach drei Bier ist er normalerweise angeheitert. c) etwas in einem anderen Licht sehen

lose – verlieren

190 a) lose b) lost c) lost

191 The correct sentences are:
a) She was angry for losing him continually in the crowd. b) She will lose every single bet. It's not her lucky day. c) I have never lost my patience as quickly as yesterday.

192 a) die Kontrolle verlieren b) den Faden verlieren c) sich nicht viele Sorgen über etwas machen d) verrückt werden e) die Geduld verlieren, wütend werden f) den Mut verlieren g) sich verlieben h) etwas aus den Augen verlieren i) nicht folgen können, nicht mitkommen j) den Kontakt mit jemandem verlieren k) sich verirren l) in Gedanken verloren sein

make – machen, tun

193 a) make b) made c) made

194 The correct sentences are:
a) He has never made a cake in his life. b) Don't make such a fuss. c) This alarm-clock is "Made in Germany" and it's broken already.

195 a) jemanden veranlassen, etwas zu tun; jemanden etwas tun lassen b) über die Runden kommen, sich nach der Decke strecken c) ein Abkommen treffen mit jemandem d) viel Aufhebens um etwas machen e) aus einer Mücke einen Elefanten machen f) jemandem schöne Augen machen g) sich mit etwas behelfen h) sich anfreunden mit jemandem i) etwas wiedergutmachen j) etwas schaffen; es schaffen, zu kommen k) das beste aus etwas machen l) etwas (eine Gelegenheit) ausnützen m) sich entschließen, eine Entscheidung treffen n) aus etwas nicht schlau werden, sich keinen Reim machen können o) jemandem die Haare zu Berge stehen lassen p) Wert auf etwas legen; sich etwas zum Prinzip machen q) auf die Tür zusteuern, schnell den Raum verlassen r) Fühl dich wie zu Hause, mach es dir bequem! s) etwas verstehen, begreifen

mean – meinen; bedeuten

196 a) means b) meant c) meant

197 The correct sentences are:
b) He meant to do her no harm but she was frightened, nevertheless. c) Do you know what this sign means?

198 a) beabsichtigen, etwas zu tun; etwas tun wollen b) es gut meinen c) es nicht böse meinen d) es ernst meinen

meet – begegnen, treffen

199 a) meet b) met c) met

200 a) We will be meeting the landlord tomorrow at 8 o'clock. b) I want to meet him again. c) The boy met his friends every day after school.

201 a) mit einer Schwierigkeit fertig werden b) jemandes Erwartungen entsprechen c) einen Unfall erleiden/haben d) Erfolg haben e) Beifall finden f) auf Ablehnung stoßen g) das Schicksal ereilt jemanden h) sterben i) den Blick erwidern j) jemanden (zufällig) treffen, wiedertreffen

pay – (be)zahlen

202 a) pay b) paid c) paid

203 a) The couple couldn't pay the rent anymore. They had to move. d) I paid for the old table with a cheque.

204 a) etwas/jemandem aufmerksam zuhören b) achten auf etwas, etwas Beachtung schenken c) es jemandem heimzahlen d) jemanden besuchen e) jemandem ein Kompliment machen f) jemandem huldigen, Anerkennung zollen g) ganz schön zahlen bei etwas, kräftig zahlen müssen, viel zu viel zahlen müssen h) ohne Verlust arbeiten, sich selbst tragen (Geschäft, Firma) i) teuer zu stehen kommen, schwer für etwas bezahlen müssen j) erfolgreich sein, sich lohnen k) sich amortisieren

put – setzen, stellen, legen

205 a) put b) put c) put

206 The correct sentences are:
a) She has put all her belongings into boxes. b) The children have put a lot of water into their sandpit. c) Please, put your suitcase in the guestroom.

207 a) etwas ein Ende bereiten, Schluß machen mit etwas b) jemanden in seine Schranken weisen c) in Worte fassen d) zunehmen (Gewicht) e) ins Fettnäpfchen treten f) ein Machtwort sprechen, energisch werden, einschreiten g) einer Sache die Krone aufsetzen, dem Faß den Boden ausschlagen h) Druck auf jemanden ausüben i) etwas richtigstellen j) jemanden beherbergen, im Haus aufnehmen als Gast k) jemandem die Schuld für etwas geben l) das Pferd von hinten aufzäumen m) sich etwas gefallen lassen, sich abfinden mit etwas n) jemandem einen Knüppel zwischen die Beine werfen, Hindernisse in den Weg legen o) erscheinen, auftauchen, aufkreuzen p) jemandem etwas (durchaus) zutrauen (im negativen Sinne) q) sich mit etwas befassen, sich etwas widmen r) in die Tat umsetzen s) jemanden beschämen (übertreffen) t) etwas aufschieben, verschieben u) abgestoßen sein von etwas v) Theater spielen, sich verstellen

read – lesen

208 a) read b) read c) read

209 a) I read about their wedding in the local paper. b) How many books can you read in a week? c) He has read all the books by Charles Dickens. d) We like to read a story to our children before they go to bed.

210 a) zwischen den Zeilen lesen b) jemanden sehr gut kennen; wissen, was jemand denkt c) ein Fach studieren d) weiterlesen e) etwas laut vorlesen f) nachlesen über etwas g) davon ausgehen können, daß . . . h) belesen sein in etwas, viel wissen über etwas

ride – reiten; fahren

211 a) rides b) rode c) ridden

212 The correct sentences are:
a) To ride an elephant you must go to India. b) Grandfather rode his pony to school when he was young. c) I haven't ridden in years. I must have forgotten everything.

213 Redewendungen:
a) seinem Steckenpferd nachgehen b) wieder dabei sein c) selig sein vor Glück, wie auf Wolken schweben d) eine riskante Sache machen e) ganz oben sein, viel Erfolg haben f) die Dinge ihren Lauf nehmen lassen g) rücksichtslos über etwas hinweggehen h) angstgepeinigt sein

rise – aufstehen; (auf)steigen

214 a) rise b) rose c) risen

215 The correct sentences are:
a) The horse tried to rise but with it's broken leg it couldn't manage. b) We both rose at once and ran into the garden. c) The moon has risen and I believe it's a full moon tonight.

216 a) sich der Lage gewachsen zeigen b) sich erheben gegen, rebellieren gegen jemanden c) von den Toten auferstehen d) Christ ist auferstanden! e) Aufstehen! Raus aus den Federn! f) erhaben sein über g) es zu etwas bringen

Merke:
Wie *rise* wird *arise* gebildet:
arise/arose/arisen - sich erheben.
Man darf es nicht verwechseln mit *raise:*
raise/raised/raised - etwas (er)heben

run – rennen, laufen

217 a) runs b) ran c) run

218 The correct sentences are:
a) He will always run faster than you. b) I dreamed that I ran and ran and never reached the house. c) When he saw her he ran as fast as he could to meet her.

219 Redewendungen:
a) jemandem zufällig begegnen, stoßen auf jemanden b) auflaufen, stranden c) ein Geschäft führen, betreiben; einen Betrieb leiten d) Besorgungen machen e) den Haushalt führen f) den Laden schmeißen g) für das Präsidentenamt kandidieren h) etwas nicht mehr haben i) etwas geht einem demnächst aus j) jemanden überfahren k) heftig, hitzig werden (Gefühle) l) Fieber haben m) das liegt in der Familie n) austrocknen o) ein Risiko eingehen p) Schulden machen q) in Schwierigkeiten geraten r) um sein Leben laufen s) an einem Wettrennen teilnehmen t) sich auf der Straße herumtreiben u) Stille Wasser sind tief.

say – sagen

220 a) say b) said c) said

221 The correct sentences are:
b) I wonder what he'll say when he hears the news. c) Has she said anything nice about me? f) How do you say "I love you" in Spanish?

222 Redewendungen:
a) gesagt, getan b) das ist leichter gesagt als getan c) es versteht sich von selbst, daß . . . d) Sag bloß! Was du nicht sagst! e) Das kannst du laut sagen! Das stimmt wirklich! Da hast du recht! f) und das will was heißen g) das heißt, vielmehr h) sagen wir mal i) ganz zu schweigen von . . . j) letzten Endes; schließlich; man darf nicht vergessen, daß . . . k) ängstlich, schüchtern sein l) das Tischgebet sprechen m) sich sagen; sich denken

see – sehen

223 a) see b) saw c) seen

224 The correct sentences are:
a) From the top of the tree I saw the village in the distance. b) I have seen him twice today. c) With that mass of hair can you see anything at all?

225 Redewendungen:
a) engstirnig sein b) sich kümmern um etwas c) jemanden loswerden, nicht mehr sehen d) mit jemandem völlig übereinstimmen e) sich persönlich von etwas überzeugen f) die Erleuchtung haben; etwas verstehen; zur Einsicht kommen; entstehen; auftreten g) sehen, woher der Wind weht; die Lage abschätzen h) jemanden nach Hause begleiten i) jemanden verabschieden j) jemanden hinausbegleiten k) in einem schlechten Zustand sein; schon mal bessere Zeiten gesehen haben l) verstehen, was jemand will/meint/denkt m) etwas zu Ende bringen n) jemandem beistehen; helfen bei etwas o) dafür sorgen, daß . . . ; darauf achten, daß . . . p) rot sehen, wütend werden, in Wut geraten q) den Wald vor lauter Bäumen nicht sehen r) Ich glaube nur, was ich mit eigenen Augen sehe. s) etwas (noch) erleben

seek – (auf)suchen; versuchen

226 a) seek b) sought c) sought

227 The correct sentences are:
b) I'll never stop to seek the meaning in life. c) She sought my help whenever she was in trouble.

228 Redewendungen:
a) sein Glück suchen b) jemandem nach dem Leben trachten c) jemanden ausfindig machen; aufs Korn nehmen d) sehr gefragt/begehrt sein; Die Präsidentin ist so gefragt, daß sie keinen Moment Ruhe hat.

sell – verkaufen

229 a) sell b) sold c) sold

230 The correct sentences are:
a) They have sold all the cheap jeans already. b) The boy is selling all sorts of strange articles. c) We couldn't get any tickets because the performance was sold out.

231 Redewendungen:
a) jemanden verraten, betrügen b) von etwas überzeugt/begeistert sein c) übers Ohr gehauen werden d) mit Verlust verkaufen e) weggehen wie warme Semmeln

send – senden, schicken

232 a) send b) sent c) sent

233 The correct sentences are:
a) Don't send me away, yet. I'd like to stay a little longer. d) I can't come to the party but I'll send you a present. f) The last time I sent a letter to him is quite a while ago.

234 Redewendungen:
a) jemanden fortjagen b) jemanden verjagen zu Boden schleudern c) jemandem eine Nachricht schicken d) einen Brief nachschicken (an eine neue Adresse)

set – setzen, stellen, legen

235 a) Set b) set c) set

236 The correct sentences are:
a) Mary set her cup down and started to laugh helplessly. c) Her mind was set on winning. She would succeed, she knew it.

237 Redewendungen:
a) jemanden freilassen b) aufbrechen; sich aufmachen nach c) eine Reise antreten d) sich vornehmen, etwas zu tun; sich an etwas machen e) etwas in Angriff nehmen f) etwas (heute) zum ersten Mal sehen g) etwas anzünden h) etwas anzünden i) eintreten j) den Wecker stellen k) einsetzen, beginnen l) Streit auslösen m) sich etwas in den Kopf setzen n) sich beruhigen o) vorbereitet für etwas sein; bereit, startklar sein p) den Ton angeben q) das Tempo angeben r) entschieden gegen etwas sein s) das Herz an etwas hängen t) entschlossen sein, etwas zu tun u) jemandem ein gutes Beispiel geben v) jemandem durch Mark und Bein gehen (bes. Geräusch) w) ein Gedicht vertonen x) den Tisch decken (vgl. lay the table)

shake – schütteln

238 a) shaking b) shook c) shaken

239 The correct sentences are:
a) It says you have to shake the juice before opening it. b) Her whole body still shook with fear. c) I think we have shaken off the police.

240 Redewendungen:
a) jemandem die Hand schütteln b) eine ungastliche Stätte mit dankbarem Gefühl verlassen c) jemandem mit der Faust drohen d) wie Espenlaub zittern e) nervös sein f) erschüttert über etwas sein g) jemanden aufrütteln h) jemandes Glauben erschüttern i) Mach mal dalli! Tempo! Beeile dich!

shed – ausgießen, vergießen

241 a) shed b) shed c) shed

242 a) Snakes shed their skin once a year. b) The oven shed a very pleasant warmth.

243 a) Licht auf eine Sache werfen; zur Aufklärung von etwas beitragen b) sich häuten (z.B. Schlange) c) ihre Blätter abwerfen (Bäume) d) eine schlechte Gewohnheit ablegen e) ein paar Pfund abnehmen f) seine Hemmungen ablegen g) jemandem keine Träne nachweinen

shine – scheinen; glänzen

244 a) will shine b) shone c) shone

245 a) Tomorrow, the sun will shine again. b) Jack polished his car until it shone. c) The light in his room is shining, he must be home.

246 a) Aufstehen! Raus aus den Federn! b) in/bei etwas glänzen; herausragend sein bei einer Sache c) eine Lampe richten auf d) sich bei jemandem anbiedern

Merke:
In der Bedeutung *polieren* wird *shined* anstatt *shone* verwendet:
He shined his shoes. - Er polierte seine Schuhe.

shoot – (er)schießen

247 a) shoots b) shot c) shot

248 a) Being in a great hurry, he shot out of the house. d) In Africa people still shoot big game.

249 a) eine bloße Vermutung b) schnelle Fortschritte machen c) sein Pulver verschossen haben; keine Argumente mehr haben d) jemanden mit Fragen bombardieren e) bei Rot über die Kreuzung fahren f) einen schnellen Blick werfen auf etwas g) einen Film machen h) sich Heroin spritzen

show – zeigen

250 a) show b) showed c) shown

251 a) Jenny has shown you how to milk the cows, hasn't she? b) I will show all my photographs at the meeting. c) They showed us what they thought quite clearly.

252 a) jemanden hereinführen b) jemanden hinausführen c) mit etwas angeben d) jemanden herumführen e) aufkreuzen; erscheinen f) die Karten offen auf den Tisch legen, aufdecken g) jemandem die Stadt zeigen h) die Zähne zeigen

shrink – einschrumpfen, einlaufen

253 a) shrink b) shrank c) shrunk

254 a) They seem to shrink into themselves when he shouts. b) Sue shrank back from her daily tasks. c) My new blanket has shrunk ten centimetres. I will make a complaint.

255 a) zurückschrecken vor etwas b) sich in sich selbst zurückziehen; Wenn sie in Gedanken verloren war, schien sie sich immer in sich selbst zurückzuziehen.

Merke:
Adjektivisch wird manchmal *shrunken* verwendet:
a shrunken hand, shrunken cheeks - abgemagert, eingefallen

shut – schließen, zumachen

256 a) shut b) shut c) shut

257 a) Shut your mouth when your are eating! b) The door banged shut. c) I'm sure they have shut the windows properly.

258 a) Halt den Mund! Sei still! b) jemandem den Mund verbieten; zum Schweigen bringen c) etwas schließen (z.B. Fabrik) d) etwas abstellen/abdrehen (z.B. Motor, Maschine, Gas, Wasser, Strom) e) abgetrennt sein, abgeschlossen sein von etwas f) die Augen vor etwas verschließen g) den Mund halten; schweigen h) sich einsperren

sing – singen

259 a) sings b) sang c) sung

260 a) The birds have sung all day long. Spring must be coming. b) Two people sang completely out of tune. c) Would you sing me a song? I'd like to hear your voice.

261 a) einen anderen Ton anschlagen b) ins gleich Horn tuten c) jemanden in den Schlaf singen d) klein beigeben; kleinlaut werden e) Lobeshymnen auf jemanden singen f) laut rufen g) lauter singen (vgl. to speak up) h) etwas/jemanden besingen i) laut und fröhlich singen

sink – (ver)sinken; (ver)senken

262 a) sink b) sank c) sunk

263 a) Relieved, she sank into their arms. b) I believe the ship is sinking fast. c) Linda had sunk into her chair exhaustedly.

264 a) in Vergessenheit geraten b) in tiefen Schlaf fallen c) in Kummer versinken d) Friß oder stirb! e) jemandem rutscht das Herz in die Hose

sit – sitzen

265 a) sit b) sat c) sat

266 a) Don't just sit around. Come and dance with me. d) We sat at the table and waited for the food to come.

267 a) die Hände in den Schoß legen b) keinen Finger rühren c) einen Sitzstreik veranstalten d) eine Prüfung machen e) zwischen zwei Stühlen sitzen f) für jemanden

aufbleiben; auf jemanden warten g) ausharren; sich nicht vom Fleck rühren; sich nicht beirren lassen; auf etwas bestehen h) aufhorchen i) gut dran sein; gut dastehen j) jemandem Modell/Porträt sitzen k) Setz dich gerade hin!

sleep – schlafen

268 a) sleeps b) slept c) slept

269 a) I long to be able to sleep as long as I like. b) Peter slept in today and missed the bus. c) Have you slept at all last night?

270 a) tiefschlafen b) durchschlafen; etwas nicht mitbekommen, nicht hören (z.B. Wecker) c) verschlafen; länger schlafen d) wie ein Murmeltier schlafen e) den Schlaf der Gerechten schlafen f) ein Problem überschlafen g) ich muß erst darüber schlafen h) einen Verdauungsschlaf halten i) seinen Rausch ausschlafen j) mit jemandem schlafen

slide – gleiten (lassen), rutschen

271 a) The slope was so steep we couldn't help sliding down. d) She loves to slide on ice, so when the lake was frozen she put on her slippery shoes and slid for an hour.

272 a) slide b) slid c) slid

273 a) in etwas hineinschlittern b) einer Sache entgehen c) etwas schleifen lassen; sich nicht um etwas kümmern; die Dinge laufen lassen d) über etwas hinweggehen; etwas umgehen (Frage, Thema); Da er meine Frage nicht beantworten wollte, ging er elegant darüber hinweg.

Merke:
a slide - Rodelbahn; Rutschbahn; Dia(positiv)

smell – riechen

274 a) smell b) smelt/smelled c) smelt/smelled

275 b) Someone must have started to cook. It smells good. c) Hanna had smelt him coming because of his new aftershave. d) Hanna had smelled him coming because of his new aftershave.

276 a) herumschnüffeln b) den Braten riechen; Lunte riechen c) etwas ‚faul' sein; nicht stimmen können d) etwas verstänkern e) Ärger kommen sehen

Merke:
to smell something up (AE) - etwas verstänkern (Zimmer)

speak – sprechen

277 a) speak b) spoke c) spoken

278 a) We haven't spoken since our quarrel last week. b) He spoke to her in a low voice. c) They will speak to us about their travels in Asia.

279 a) Taten zählen mehr als Worte. b) wenn man vom Teufel spricht c) ganz zu schweigen von d) nichts Nennenswertes; nicht der Rede wert e) sozusagen f) offen die Meinung sagen g) pausenlos sprechen h) gut/schlecht von jemandem sprechen i) einander böse sein; nicht mehr miteinander sprechen

spend – verbringen, ausgeben

280 a) spend b) spent c) spent

281 a) This woman spent half of her life in a foreign country. b) You have spent all your money already? I don't believe it. c) Let's spend some time together, shall we?

282 a) Alle meine Energien sind aufgebraucht. b) Es ist sinnvoll ausgegebenes Geld, die Ausgabe hat sich gelohnt. c) ausgebrannt sein, kein Geld mehr haben

spread – (sich) ausbreiten, verbreiten

283 a) spread b) spread c) spread

284 b) This weed has spread all over the place. d) For our picnic we will spread two blankets on the grass.

285 a) sich wie ein Lauffeuer verbreiten b) versuchen, auf eigenen Beinen zu stehen; ein neues Leben anfangen c) sich viel Mühe machen als Gastgeber, sich sehr anstrengen

spring – springen, sprudeln

286 a) springs b) sprang c) sprung

287 a) The door sprang open but no one was to be seen. b) Where did this rumour spring from? c) I have sprung from that cliff there.

288 a) ins Auge springen b) aufspringen c) plötzlich mit Leben erfüllt werden d) herkommen; herrühren von; abstammen von e) bei jemandem mit einer Neuigkeit herausplatzen, jemandem etwas eröffnen f) plötzlich entstehen, aufkommen

Merke:
Im AE ist auch die Form *sprung* für past tense üblich!

stand – stehen

289 a) stand b) stood c) stood

290 a) I can't see a thing if he stands in front of me. b) Look at the clouds! We stand a good chance of getting some rain later. c) All seats were taken, so she stood during the whole journey.

291 a) Ihm stehen die Haare zu Berge b) herumstehen c) eine gute Chance haben d) zu jemandem stehen; beistehen e) hart bleiben, unnachgiebig sein f) stehen für; bedeuten g) jemanden vertreten; für jemanden einspringen h) eintreten für jemanden i) jemandem die Stirn bieten j) angehen gegen jemanden/etwas k) jemanden sitzen lassen l) auf Etikette achten m) herausragen; hervorragen n) auf seiner Meinung beharren o) zusammenhalten p) eine Sache durchstehen; die Folgen tragen müssen q) auf seine Rechte pochen r) jemandem einen Drink spendieren s) siegen oder untergehen t) mit jemandem gut stehen u) eine Sache umdrehen, auf den Kopf stellen v) eine Probe bestehen w) das sieht ja ein Blinder x) es ist ganz logisch, daß. . . y) und dabei bleibt es

steal – stehlen

292 a) steals b) stole c) stolen

293 a) Never try to steal out of his presence. He'll always notice. b) They have stolen all the jewellery out of the safe. c) She never stole anything in her life.

294 a) sich davonstehlen b) jemandem den Wind aus den Segeln nehmen; jemandem die Lorbeeren stehlen c) einen verstohlenen Blick werfen auf jemanden/etwas d) jemandem ein Schnippchen schlagen, zuvorkommen e) jemandem die Schau stehlen f) stehlen; klauen; Sie bekamen nie Taschengeld, so daß sie klauten, wo immer sie auch hinkamen.

stick – stecken; kleben

295 a) Stick b) stuck c) stuck

296 a) I talked to her, but suddenly she stuck her tongue out at me. b) The twins always stick together. c) We were stuck with him and could hardly stand it.

297 a) in der Nähe bleiben; dableiben b) vor nichts zurückschrecken; keine Skrupel haben c) intensiv weiterarbeiten an etwas d) zu jemandem halten; treu bleiben e) festsitzen; nicht mehr weiterkönnen; steckenbleiben f) in jemanden vernarrt sein g) jemanden/etwas am Hals haben h) hervorstehen i) das sieht ja ein Blinder (vgl. to stand out a mile) j) etwas durchhalten, durchstehen k) unangenehm auffallen; hervorstechen l) im Gedächtnis haften bleiben m) bei der Sache bleiben n) an jemandem wie eine Klette hängen o) seinen Prinzipien treu bleiben p) sich an die Regeln halten q) ein Risiko eingehen r) die Nase in eine Sache stecken s) Hände hoch!

strike – schlagen

298 a) strikes b) struck c) struck

299 b) That tree is all black. It must have been struck by lightning. d) Every quarter of the hour the church clock strikes loudly.

300 a) jemandem einen Schlag versetzen b) einen Handel abschließen; eine Vereinbarung treffen c) ein Streichholz anzünden d) jemandem ins Auge fallen e) plötzlich zu Geld kommen; das große Los ziehen f) etwas an der Wurzel treffen g) zu einem Kompromiß kommen h) das Eisen schmieden, solange es noch heiß ist i) ins Ge-

spräch kommen; ein Gespräch anknüpfen j) Erinnert dich das an etwas? k) den richtigen Ton treffen l) sich im Ton vergreifen; sich daneben benehmen

sweat – schwitzen

301 a) sweats b) sweat/sweated c) sweat/sweated

302 b) How ever hard she worked, she never sweat one drop. c) How ever hard she worked, she never sweated one drop. e) She made me sit there for one hour. I really had to sweat it out.

303 a) Blut und Wasser schwitzen; sich abrackern für etwas b) durchhalten c) jemanden schuften lassen, ausbeuten d) jemanden schwitzen lassen

sweep – fegen, kehren

304 a) sweeps b) swept c) swept

305 a) This year our chimney has already been swept twice. b) You must sweep the broken glass away before someone steps into it.

306 a) einem in den Sinn kommen b) beiseite schieben, ignorieren (z.B. Argumente, Ratschläge; Einwände) c) jemanden mitreißen; ‚umhauen'; überwältigen d) etwas mitreißen, umreißen, fortreißen e) jemandes Zweifel ausräumen f) etwas zu verbergen suchen; unter den Teppich kehren g) Neue Besen kehren gut.

swim – schwimmen

307 a) swims b) swam c) swum

308 a) Some dogs like to swim but ours doesn't at all. b) My brother already swam like a fish at the age of four. c) We have swum the whole day, yesterday.

309 a) mit dem Strom schwimmen; sich der Mehrheit anschließen b) gegen den Strom schwimmen c) im Geld schwimmen d) vor den Augen verschwimmen

take – bringen; nehmen

310 a) takes b) took c) taken

311 a) Please, take me to a football match. b) Who has taken my books? I need them now. c) She took three pills because she felt very sick.

312 a) überrascht/verblüfft sein b) eingenommen sein von etwas c) nach jemandem geraten; ähnlich sein d) eine Pause machen e) etwas übelnehmen f) etwas für bare Münze nehmen g) sein Glück versuchen h) eine Vorliebe entwickeln für etwas; einen Gefallen finden an etwas i) etwas ins Herz schließen j) etwas als selbstverständlich ansehen/hinnehmen k) sich ein Herz fassen; Mut fassen l) sich etwas zu Herzen nehmen m) jemanden irreführen, betrügen n) sich etwas anschauen o) sich aus dem Staub machen; die Beine in die Hand nehmen p) sich Notizen machen;

mitschreiben q) etwas beachten r) Anstoß nehmen an etwas s) stattfinden t) sich verabschieden u) sich Zeit lassen v) jemanden beim Wort nehmen w) jemanden mit jemandem verwechseln x) in Kraft treten (Gesetz, Vorschrift) y) Mach, was du willst! z) auf die Schippe genommen werden aa) jemandem den Wind aus den Segeln nehmen bb) zum Trinker werden cc) sich mit jemandem abwechseln dd) Das kannst du mir glauben! Das sag' ich dir! Verlaß dich drauf! ee) Das übertrifft alles! Jetzt schlägt's aber dreizehn! ff) Nimm's leicht!

Merke:
Wie *take* wird *overtake* gebildet: overtake/overtook/overtaken - überholen

teach – lehren, unterrichten

313 a) teaches b) tought c) tought

314 b) He tought Spanish and Biology. c) I'd like to teach small children to read and write. e) My teacher has tought me many useful things.

315 a) jemandem eine Lektion erteilen (vgl. to learn a lesson) b) Das wird dir eine Lehre sein!

Merke:
You can't teach an old dog new tricks. - Was Hänschen nicht lernt, lernt Hans nimmermehr.

tell – sagen, erzählen

316 a) tell b) told c) told

317 a) Will you tell me how to get to your place, please. b) They never told me anything. I had to find it out myself. c) If you tell him what I have just told you I'll never speak a word to you again.

318 a) etwas hinausposaunen b) jemanden ausschimpfen, schelten c) jemandem etwas ins Gesicht sagen d) flunkern e) es ist schwer zu sagen f) man kann nie wissen g) Du sagst es! Wem sagen Sie das? h) Das glaube ich dir nicht! Das glaubst du doch selbst nicht! i) Ich kann ihnen versichern, daß. . .

think – denken

319 a) think b) thought c) thought

320 a) What do you think you are doing? Stop it at once! d) Certainly, he has thought of everything. e) When I was a child I never thought I'd grow up.

321 a) seinen Entschluß ändern; sich umentscheiden; sich etwas anders überlegen b) etwas für angemessen halten, für richtig halten c) sich etwas überlegen d) sich etwas gründlich überlegen e) wenn ich es mir recht überlege; da fällt mir ein; übrigens f) das habe ich mir gedacht g) Denkste! h) große Stücke halten auf jemanden i) eine hohe Meinung von jemandem haben; viel von jemandem halten j) etwas ersinnen, aushecken

throw – werfen

322 a) Throw b) threw c) thrown

323 a) Yesterday, I threw myself onto the sofa b) Her father had thrown her old jeans in the bin. She was furious. c) The horse tried to throw him but he stayed in the saddle.

324 a) sich jemandem an den Hals werfen b) jemandem etwas vorwerfen c) alle Vorsicht in den Wind schlagen d) einen Wutanfall bekommen e) ganz in einer Sache aufgehen; mit Leib und Seele dabei sein f) etwas einwerfen; einstreuen; hinzufügen (Bemerkung) g) sich intensiv mit einer Sache beschäftigen h) Zweifel an etwas aufkommen lassen i) Licht auf eine Sache werfen j) etwas schlecht machen; einer Sache einen Dämpfer aufsetzen k) das Handtuch werfen l) die Flinte ins Korn werfen m) jemanden abschütteln, loswerden n) etwas über Bord/ über den Haufen werfen o) sich übergeben p) sich aufspielen q) Das hat mich glatt umgehauen!

understand – verstehen

325 a) understand b) understood c) understood

326 a) If you try, you'll understand what I'm explaining. b) I understood what he wanted immediately – only, I didn't want to give it to him.

327 a) das versteht sich von selbst b) Ich nehme an, daß. . .; Ich höre, daß. . . c) Was verstehen Sie darunter?

win – gewinnen

328 a) win b) won c) won

329 b) Who do you think will win? c) My father was extremely proud when I won the first prize in the contest.

330 a) sich Ruhm erwerben b) ohne Anstrengung gewinnen; leicht gewinnen c) jemandes Herz/Liebe gewinnen d) den Sieg davontragen e) das eigene Brot verdienen f) jemanden für etwas gewinnen g) Ok, du hast recht; ich gebe auf

write – schreiben

331 a) write b) wrote c) written

332 a) In March I will write four tests in a row. b) All the instructions are written on this slip of paper. c) Not knowing the answer I wrote a lot of nonsense.

333 a) Das ist nichts besonderes; Das ist nicht so toll b) in den Wind geschrieben, vergänglich c) etwas ‚abschreiben', vergessen können, nicht mehr benutzen können d) stenographieren e) jemanden beschreiben als f) schriftlich etwas anfordern g) etwas anpreisen, rühmen; etwas nachtragen